THE CENTER FOR MIND & ESTEEM DEVELOPMENT, INC.

POWER CONSCIOUS

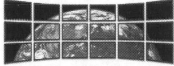

THINK MY POTENTIAL MY POSSIBILITY

- INTENTION
- DECISION
- REALIZATION
- ATTITUDE
- SURRENDER

BY MARVIN MACK
YOUR PERSONAL & PROFESSIONAL DEVELOPMENT

THE CENTER FOR MIND & ESTEEM DEVELOPMENT, INC.

RE-FOCUS: SUCCESS IS NOW

SELF-EMPOWERMENT

- CHANGING FROM WITHIN
- MY ENERGY
- MY BARRIERS
- SELF-LOVE
- BELIEVING IN MYSELF

BY MARVIN MACK
YOUR PERSONAL DEVELOPMENT COACH

THE CENTER FOR MIND & ESTEEM DEVELOPMENT, INC.

YOU, INC.

FOR PROFESSIONAL ADVANCEMENT

- LEADERSHIP
- SELF-MANAGEMENT
- PROFESSIONALISM
- QUALITY SERVICE
- TEAM BUILDING

BY MARVIN MACK
YOUR PROFESSIONAL DEVELOPMENT COACH

Power Conscious - Re-Focus: Success Is Now - You, Inc.

Affirm:

I Am Powerful Enough

To Fulfill My Purpose and Achieve
the Love, Joy, Peace & Great Riches
I Truly Desire and Deserve!

Daily Renewal

BY MARVIN MACK
YOUR PERSONAL & PROFESSIONAL
DEVELOPMENT COACH

THE CENTER FOR MIND & ESTEEM DEVELOPMENT, INC.

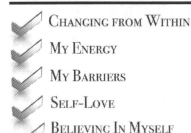

Affirm: I Am Powerful Enough
To Fulfill My Purpose and Achieve the Love, Joy, Peace
& Great Riches I Truly Desire and Deserve!

iUniverse
1663 Liberty Drive
Bloomington, IN 47403
www.iuniverse.com
1-800-Authors (1-800-288-4677)

Because of the dynamic nature of the Internet, any Web addresses or links contained in this book may have changed since publication and may no longer be valid. The views expressed in this work are solely those of the author and do not necessarily reflect the views of the publisher, and the publisher hereby disclaims any responsibility for them.

ISBN: 978-1-4401-9989-9 (sc)
ISBN: 978-1-4401-9990-5 (dj)
ISBN: 978-1-4401-9991-2 (ebk)

Printed in the United States of America

iUniverse rev. date: 03/30/2010

The Center For Mind & Esteem Development, Inc.

Power Conscious

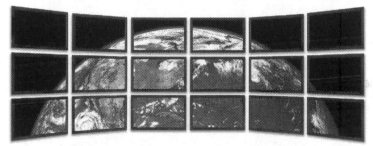

Think My Potential My Possibility

Intention

Decision

Realization

Attitude

Surrender

by Marvin Mack

Your Personal & Professional Development

BONUS Membership Website: iampowerfulenough.com
Download Additional Self-Help eBooks, Audios & Videos FREE

Personal Development - Your eBook Library

Warning! If it is our deepest intent to achieve more health, romance, professional advancement or wealth, then we must first Empower ourselves. This library is designed to empower us to unload our negative thinking/baggage and begin thinking about our potential and possibility. This will empower us to begin tapping into a higher power to overcome life challenges in order to create the life we ultimately desire and deserve.

 The 7 Habits of Highly Effective People by Steven R. Covey - This book will empower you to develop powerful habits that will support you in achieving your next level of success.

 The Science of Being Great by Wallace D. Wattes "Any Person Can Become Great" - This book will empower you to develop the mind set that will support you in overcoming your life challenges achieving your ultimate goals and desires.

 Law Of Attraction - The Law of Attraction: The Secret to Fulfilling Your Heart's Desires Without Ever Leaving the Privacy of Your Own Mind is a simple but powerful book that will empower you to begin attracting and drawing to yourself people, situations and circumstances you need in order to create the ultimate lifestyle you truly desire to live.

 The Little Book of Ultimate Power "Cure Fear, Build Confidence, Find Success" - Discover how to change your life. This up-to-date guide teaches you how to cure fear, achieve your dream, build confidence, find success and much more.

 SAVE YOUR MARRIAGE "And Develop A Lifelong Love!" - To Find the Solution, First See the Problem! In this piece, you will be guided through the process of recognizing the problems which you are encountering before attempting a solution.

And Much More ...

Table of Contents

THE CENTER FOR MIND & ESTEEM DEVELOPMENT, INC.

RE-FOCUS: SUCCESS IS NOW

SELF-EMPOWERMENT

CHANGING FROM WITHIN

MY ENERGY

MY BARRIERS

SELF-LOVE

BELIEVING IN MYSELF

BY MARVIN MACK
YOUR PERSONAL DEVELOPMENT COACH

BONUS Membership Website: iampowerfulenough.com
Download Additional Self-Help eBooks, Audios & Videos FREE

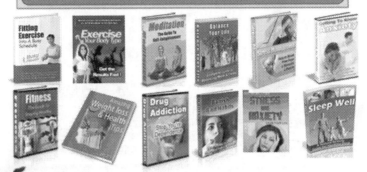

Wellness Center - Your eBook Library

It Is A Fact that success means nothing if our health is failing. If it is our intent to materialize successful romantic relationships, professional advancement or financial wealth, then our #1 goal must be to develop a healthier stronger mind, body and spirit. At this level of empowerment not only are we strong enough to overcome life challenges to succeed, but we are more open and receptive to attracting and drawing to ourselves our true goals and desires.

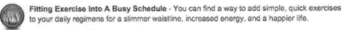

Fitting Exercise Into A Busy Schedule - You can find a way to add simple, quick exercises to your daily regimens for a slimmer waistline, increased energy, and a happier life.

Amazing Weight Loss & Health Tips and Discover 100 Ways to Lose 10 Pounds, Feel Better & Become Healthier ... - What you should always do before you sit down to eat if you really want to lose weight fast! What foods are good to eat -- and what foods you should stay away from at all costs!

Banish Bad Habits - How to free Yourself From Bad Habits, Forever - You'll learn how to replace your bad habits with healthy new habits. Focusing on your new lifestyle is like freeing the hand tied behind your back—suddenly you have power to bring about the change you desire.

Stress Management- How To Break Free From a Stressful Life - Do you really want to go through the rest of your life feeling "stressed out?" Do you like the idea of feeling "out of control" and that everything in life is a trial? Perhaps it is time for you to confront this situation and seek help to restore some sort of balance in your life and break free from this cycle.

Balance Your Life - Is your life out of balance? If so, then the book, 'Balance Your Life - The Complete Guide to Managing Work and Family', is definitely something you need!

And Much More ...

Table of Contents

Copyright © by Marvin Mack
The Center For Mind & Esteem Development, Inc.
15 Charles Plaza
Baltimore, MD 21201
Iampowerfulenough.com
410-385-8978

THE CENTER FOR MIND & ESTEEM DEVELOPMENT, INC.

YOU, INC.

FOR PROFESSIONAL ADVANCEMENT

LEADERSHIP

SELF-MANAGEMENT

PROFESSIONALISM

QUALITY SERVICE

TEAM BUILDING

BY MARVIN MACK
YOUR PROFESSIONAL DEVELOPMENT COACH

BONUS Membership Website: iampowerfulenough.com
Download Additional Self-Help eBooks,
Audios & Videos FREE

Your Virtual Online Training Courses

You, Inc. Table of Contents

Affirm:

I Am Powerful Enough

To Fulfill My Purpose and Achieve
the Love, Joy, Peace & Great Riches
I Truly Desire and Deserve!

Daily Renewal

BY MARVIN MACK
YOUR PERSONAL & PROFESSIONAL
DEVELOPMENT COACH

THE CENTER FOR MIND & ESTEEM DEVELOPMENT, INC.

Table of Contents

Introduction

Make a commitment to yourself to take time each day for your Personal and Professional Development. (PPD) The ultimate goal of this document is to assist you in discovering the power within you to fulfill your purpose and materialize your deepest goals and desires.

(PPD) addresses the major skills gaps that we need to fill in order to fulfill our purpose and achieve our deepest goals and desires. It provides you with important questions that you must ask and answer for yourself. Moreover, PPD provide a breakthrough in the technology of human potential. Implementing and re-enforcing its simple but powerful concepts will have you time, energy and money. In addition, PPD will dramatically increase your self-esteem, self-confidence and self-worth and value. Moreover, it will increase motivation, presentation and communication, productivity and overall quality of life.

If your intent is to advance personally and professionally, I highly recommend that you incorporate a PPD program into your daily life as a strategy for growth and development. It will serve to evaluate your strengths and weaknesses. Moreover, PPD provides the self-empowerment information you need to build on your strengths and correct your weaknesses. It will allow you to develop your critical thinking skills, emotional fortitude and the power consciousness required to create the power life you truly desire and deserve.

Preface

In 1996, I stared The Center For Mind and Esteem Development (CMED) for two reasons. First, because it was revealed to me that my life's purpose is to uplift the consciousness of the world. Second, I wanted to bring the concepts of Personal and Professional Development to people who could not afford it, or otherwise would not be exposed to it. I grew up in poverty, but as a young man I was exposed to metaphysical concepts, as well as personal and professional development. After seeing how much these concepts healed and transformed my life, I was compelled to share this information with the world.

After starting the company in 1996, I walked into Housing Authority of Baltimore City Resident Services with a proposal in hand and said to the Director, "Give me the people and I will help them to transform their lives." With reservation, they allowed me to do a 30-day Personal and Professional Development pilot program. The pilot was a major success and 14 years later they are still one of my top clients.

Since then, we have been teaching the core principles of this book to state agencies, non-profits, and private companies increasing their productivity, level of professional, and overall quality of life. Moreover, we have provided coaching sessions to assist directors, manager, counselors and supervisors on how to effectively connect with and influence their members and customers in a positive manner.

The Center For Mind And Esteem Development, Inc. is a training institute committed to human development and individual achievement. Our goal is to teach self-empowerment principles to all people so that they can reach their fullest potential, fulfill their life's purpose, and achieve their personal and professional goals.

The World Has Changed!

The world is undergoing radical change. Our lives and the workforce are more demanding and challenging. As technology and globalization becomes more pervasive, competition is dramatically increasing and people will be required to learn, know and do more in less time. Are we prepared?

Success Now

The Center For Mind & Esteem Development, Inc. has concluded that the success of any family unit or work/business environment is dependent on the empowerment of each person in that unit.

This course is designed to empower you to develop the mind set required to:

> Focus, execute, meet deadlines and achieve goals.

> Present and communicate confidently and effectively.

> React and respond to negative challenges in a powerful manner.

> Be mentally, emotionally, spiritually and physically strong enough to handle challenges, such as: multiple projects, crises and difficult people.

> Give quality service in a professional manner to succeed now.

> Communicate effectively in all relationships.

> Develop stronger relationships with all people and be a powerful team player.

The Center For Mind & Esteem Development, Inc. has developed this innovative course to teach the skills of Self-Empowerment. Self-Empowerment is a specific set of beliefs and behaviors that individuals and companies need to master in order to Grow and Succeed in a changing world. It is a discipline of its own. CMED, Inc. uses a holistic approach to teach the skill of self-empowerment.

CMED, Inc. Methodology: "Take responsibility for your own Life!"
We aim to empower you to transform your own life by:

➢ Helping you to clearly define your purpose, goals and desires for success.

➢ Assisting you in identifying your personal barriers to success.

➢ Exposing you to some of the most powerful self-empowerment information in the world.

➢ Giving you simple practical techniques for overcoming your barriers, energy drainers and life challenges in order to succeed.

➢ Allowing you to choose to use the self-empowerment principles and techniques in your daily life or not.

Personal & Professional Development challenges you to ask and answer the following questions for yourself:

1. **What is your true purpose in this world?**

2. **What exactly do you desire? What are you hungry for?**

3. **What do you need to heal and transform within yourself in order to powerfully fulfill your purpose and accomplish your goals and desires?**

4. **What mechanisms do you have in order to overcome your life challenges in order to succeed?**

5. **Do you believe and have confidence in yourself?**

Affirm: I Am Powerful Enough is your 21 Century Handbook For Success. It consist of four simple but powerful Books/Courses:

1. **I Am Powerful – 13 Daily Renewals**
2. **Power Conscious for Personal Growth and Development**
3. **Re-Focus: Success Is Now for Present Time**
4. **You, Inc. for Professional Advancement**

As your personal and professional development coach, I encourage you to take 30 or more minutes each day to develop your mind, body and spirit. These books will assist you. **Also, you may take advantage of our Bonus Website. Here you will find addition Self-Improvement eBooks, Audios, Videos & Your Virtual Coach. Just log into:**

iampowerfulenough.com
Login: iampowerful
Pass Code: selflove

THE CENTER FOR MIND & ESTEEM DEVELOPMENT, INC.

POWER CONSCIOUS

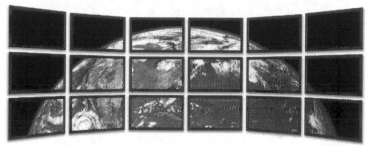

THINK MY POTENTIAL MY POSSIBILITY

INTENTION

DECISION

REALIZATION

ATTITUDE

SURRENDER

BY MARVIN MACK
YOUR PERSONAL & PROFESSIONAL DEVELOPMENT

BONUS Membership Website: iampowerfulenough.com
Download Additional Self-Help eBooks, Audios & Videos FREE

Personal Development - Your eBook Library

Warning! If it is our deepest intent to achieve more health, romance, professional advancement or wealth, then we must first Empower ourselves. This library is designed to empower us to unload our negative thinking/baggage and begin thinking about our potential and possibility. This will empower us to begin tapping into a higher power to overcome life challenges in order to create the life we ultimately desire and deserve.

 The 7 Habits of Highly Effective People by Steven R. Covey - This book will empower you to develop powerful habits that will support you in achieving your next level of success.

 The Science of Being Great by Wallace D. Wattes "Any Person Can Become Great" - This book will empower you to develop the mind set that will support you in overcoming your life challenges achieving your ultimate goals and desires.

 Law Of Attraction - The Law of Attraction: The Secret to Fulfilling Your Heart's Desires Without Ever Leaving the Privacy of Your Own Mind is a simple but powerful book that will empower you to begin attracting and drawing to yourself people, situations and circumstances you need in order to create the ultimate lifestyle you truly desire to live.

 The Little Book of Ultimate Power "Cure Fear, Build Confidence, Find Success" - Discover how to change your life. This up-to-date guide teaches you how to cure fear, achieve your dream, build confidence, find success and much more.

 SAVE YOUR MARRIAGE "And Develop A Lifelong Love!" - To Find the Solution, First See the Problem! In this piece, you will be guided through the process of recognizing the problems which you are encountering before attempting a solution.

And Much More ...

Table of Contents

5 Power Conscious Daily Renewals

Intention

Who do you desire to be and what do you desire to create with the rest of your life?

Health - Power Conscious Goal #1:

> **I intend to achieve a healthier, stronger mind, body and spirit.**

Relationships - Power Conscious Goal #2.

> **I intend to create successful relationships with all people, both personally and professionally.**

Professional Advancement - Power Conscious Goal #3:

> **I intend to achieve professional advancement.**

Financial Wealth - Power Conscious Goal #4:

> **I intend to achieve financial wealth.**

Authentic Success - Power Conscious Goal #5:

> **I intend to achieve the love, joy, peace and great riches I truly desire and deserve.**

Decide Now

1. I decide now to **look beyond negative appearances** and seek the truth. Mastering this concept will empower me to discover how profoundly powerful I am to transform negative appearances into positive truths.

2. I decide now to **relax and be patient** with myself and people, while at the same time, doing what must be done in order to materialize my deepest goals and desires. Mastering this concept will empower me to re-energize, think more clearly and take the necessary action steps required in order to achieve my daily objectives.

3. I decide now to **listen to my intuition** and follow through on what it tells me to do. This will allow me to tap into a higher level of intelligence in order to materialize my deepest goals and desires.

4. I decide now to **take back the power** that I have given to negative people, situations or circumstances. Mastering this concept will allow me to re-focus my time, energy and thoughts on materializing my highest potential and possibility. I now realize that I have the power enough to fulfill my purpose and create a great life.

5. I decide now to **take risks and never give up** on discovering how profoundly powerful I am to set goals and do what must be done in order to bring those goals into physical manifestation. I am powerful enough. I am Powerful enough to make effective decisions that will support me in materializing my deepest goals and desires.

5 Realizations for Action

Moving from an Understanding to Action

1. **I now realize that I must** Operate At My Highest Potential **on a daily basis in order to grow and develop my mind, body and spirit.**

2. **I realize that I must** Think Powerfully **in order to overcome my life challenges to Succeed.**

3. **I now realize that I must** Believe and have Confidence **in my ability to "do what must be done" in order to successfully complete my daily objectives.**

4. **I now realize that I must** Make Effective Decisions **on a daily basis. This will support the achievement of my deepest goals and desires.**

5. **I now realize that I must** Take Action Now **if my deepest intent is to materialize my personal and professional goals and desires.**

At this level of Power Conscious thinking, ultimately you will be motivated to discover the power within to "Do What Must Be Done" in order to materialize your goals and desires.

5 Power Conscious Attitudes For Success Now
I Can! I Will! It is Done!
I Give Thanks!

1. I can and I will **forgive myself and other people** for any wrongdoings. This will allow me to be open and receptive to Healing and Transforming my life beyond my wildest dreams. I Give Thanks!

2. I can and I will **believe and have confidence in my ability to operate at my highest potential** in order to create love, joy, peace and great riches on this earth. I Give Thanks!

3. I can and I will **react and respond to life powerfully,** regardless of what life puts before me. This will empower me to react and respond to life powerfully in order to create the great life I truly desire and deserve. Not just for myself, but for all the people on this planet. I Give Thanks!

4. I can and I will **stop allowing negative people, situations and circumstances to drain my energy** and take me off focus. I will re-focus that energy on realizing my highest potential to materialize my deepest goals and desires. I Give Thanks!

5. I can and I will **attract into my life positive people, situations and circumstances** that reflect and support my deepest goals and desires. In addition, I can and I will attract the love, joy, peace and great riches I truly desire and deserve. I Give Thanks!

I Surrender To My Higher Power

I Surrender To A Higher Power Within Myself

BE STILL AND KNOW THAT I AM POWERFUL

I am open and receptive to **discovering a higher power** within myself in order to achieve my highest Potential and Possibility.

I **forgive myself and other people** for any wrongdoings; therefore, I am free from guilt, shame and resentment.

I am open and receptive to **learning all that life has to teach** me, so that I am a stronger, more powerful person.

I am open and receptive to using my inner power to **heal and transform** my life to achieve my heart's desires.

I am open and receptive to overcoming my life challenges to **achieve the love, joy, peace and great riches** I truly desire and deserve.

I am open and receptive to overcoming my fears, doubts and insecurities, to **do what must be done** in order to **manifest my desires.**

I am open and receptive to **being a powerful person** to give great service and achieve my personal and professional goals and desires.

I Surrender To A Higher Power Within Myself!
BE STILL AND KNOW THAT I AM POWERFUL
I Give Thanks. I Give Thanks. I Give Thanks.

Power Conscious – A Command to Visualize & Produce Your Highest Potential and Possibility

How to Get What You Want

"There is something in the man who succeeds, which enables him to use his faculties successfully, and this something must be cultivated by all who succeed; the question is, what is it?

It is hard to find a word, which shall express it, and not be misleading. This something is Poise; and poise is peace and power combined; but is more than poise, for poise is a condition, and this something is an action as well as a condition. This Something is Faith; but it is more than faith, as faith is commonly understood: As commonly understood, faith consists of the action of believing things which cannot be proved; and the Something which causes success is more than that. It is Conscious Power in Action.

It is Active Power-Consciousness. Power-Consciousness is what you feel when you know that you can do a thing; and you know How to do the thing. If I can cause you to Know that you can succeed, and to know that you know How to succeed, I have placed success within your grasp; for if you know that you can do a thing and know that you know how to do it, it is impossible that you should fail to do it, if you really try. When you are in full Power Consciousness, you will approach the task in an absolutely successful frame of mind. Every thought will be a successful thought, every action a successful action, and if every thought and action is successful, the sum-total of all your actions cannot be failure."

The Science of Getting Rich
The Proven Mental Program To A Life of Wealth
By Wallace D. Wattles

I read hundreds of books, listened to tons of audiotapes, attended countless seminars, and exposed myself to scores of successful people, concepts and methodologies on the topic of success. In the final analysis of my research, I have discovered that 1) Success is a self-discovery process and 2) one must access a Power Consciousness in order to materialize success on any level. I have discovered that accessing a Power Consciousness is the key to every motivational, inspirational, self-help, business or professional growth and development process.

Each of us has the opportunity to access our Power Consciousness in order to heal and transform our lives and materialize great success. If you truly desire to heal and transform your life in order to materialize more health, relationships, career advancement and financial wealth, you must begin by accessing your Power Conscious.

The information in this program is not merely motivational. It will empower you to access the Power Conscious mindset based on where you are in your life, right now. You will learn that no matter who you are or where you are in your life right now, accessing your Power Consciousness will dramatically increase your ability to overcome life challenges to succeed in life.

Who do you desire to be and what do you desire to materialize in your life? In the chapters that follow, we will give you the self-empowerment tools you need to access your Power Conscious mindset. This will allow you to discover the power within in order to be who you desire to be, fulfill your purpose and materialize your deepest goals and desires.

In the chapters that follow, I will introduce you to 5 major components of Power Conscious. Each of the components focuses on fundamental principles of personal and professional development. The theme that runs through each component /success principle is "I Am Powerful Enough to be who I desire to be and materialize my deepest goals and desires. I can, I will, and it is done. I give thanks." With just this simple concept, you will go to your next level of success again and again. You will heal and transform your life and the lives of the people around you. Here is a brief description of each Power Conscious principle for success.

5 Power Conscious Principles in a Nutshell:

Success Principle #1: Intention - something that someone plans to do or achieve – the quality or state of having a purpose in mind. Our intention is our purpose and our deepest personal and professional goals and desires. After clarifying and confirming our deepest goals and desires for success now, we must visualize them and write a personal mission statement. Having a personal and professional vision and mission statement is critical to our next level of success. This chapter will motivate and inspire you to clarify and confirm your goals and desires for success now.

Success Principle #2: Decision - something that someone chooses or makes up his or her mind about, after considering it and other possible choices. After clarifying our intention, we must make a conscious decision to succeed. When we affirm a decision, we send out a powerful energy into the universe. The universe will then align the exact forces we need in order to bring about our desired success. I will offer you 5 Power Conscious Decisions For Success Now that will allow you, right now, to align the exact forces you need to materialize your deepest goals and desires. This will empower you to eliminate indecision, procrastination and uncertainty to act and produce powerful results in your life.

Success Principle #3: Realization - to know, understand and accept. Once we are clear on our intent and have made a decision to succeed, when we *keep meeting the temporary defeat*, it may mean that we need to come to a higher realization. Here, we will explore some elements that we may need to heal and transform within ourselves in order to materialize successful results. I will offer you 5 Power Conscious Realizations for Success Now. These insights are designed to save us time, energy and thought. By developing this success principle, we will become better prepared to effectively deal with setbacks, disappointments and problems.

Success Principle #4: Attitude - an expression or general feeling about something, a physical posture, either conscious or unconscious, especially while interacting with others. Developing and maintaining a positive attitude is crucial to the process of achieving success. I will offer you 5 Power Conscious Attitudes for Success Now. This will empower you to rise above negative people, situations and circumstances. In addition, a positive attitude will help you to feel better, look better and produce better results. In addition, it will empower you to effectively overcome your life challenges to fulfill your purpose and materialize your goals and desires in a positive manner.

Success Principle #5: Surrender - an act of willing submission to your higher power. No one materializes true greatness in their life by their own human consciousness. Materializing true greatness is a direct effect of surrendering to a higher power or divine intelligence. If it is our deepest intent to materialize greatness in our lives, then we must consciously surrender to a higher power within ourselves. In this chapter, I will offer you a simple but powerful meditation. This will empower you to develop your belief and confidence in a higher power greater than yourself to fulfill your purpose and materialize your deepest goals and desires.

My 21st Century Goals For Success Now

1. My Mind, Body and Spirit:

    a. My Mind _____

    b. My Body _____

    c. My Spirit _____

2. My Relationships (Personal & Professional)

    a. My Relationship with Myself

    _____

    b. My Relationship with Family

    _____

    c. My Professional Relationships

    _____

    d. My Relationship with the World

    _____

3. Professional Advancement

    a. Technical Skills

    _____

    b. Presentation & Communication Skills

    _____

    c. Team Building Skills

    _____

    d. Customer Service Skills

    _____

4. Financial Wealth

    a. Annual Financial Goal

    _____

    b. Wealth - What do you want to Buy In Cash by this date _____?

    _____

Intention - 5 Power Conscious Goals For Success Now

Who do you desire to be and what do you desire to create with the rest of your life?

Health - Goal #1:

I intend to achieve a healthier, stronger mind, body and spirit.

Relationships - Goal #2:

I intend to create successful relationships with all people, both personally and professionally.

Professional Advancement - Goal #3:

I intend to achieve professional advancement.

Financial Wealth - Goal #4:

I intend to achieve financial wealth.

Authentic Success - Goal #5:

I intend to achieve the love, joy, peace and great riches I truly desire and deserve.

Intention

What is your purpose? Who do you desire to be and what do you desire to materialize in your life? Ask yourself, now "What is my purpose? Who do I desire to be and what are my personal and professional goals and desires? What is my intent at this point in my life?"

If we truly desire to succeed in life, if you truly desire to fulfill our purpose, if we truly desire to materialize more Health, Relationships, Professional Advancement or Wealth, if we truly desire to overcome life challenges to materialize more love, joy, peace and great riches, **then we must be crystal clear on our INTENTION.** One of the major reasons that we do not succeed in life is because we do not know who we are, our purpose and what we truly desire in our lives. And this is only because we have not taken the time to sit down and ask ourselves the questions, "Who do I desire to be, what is my purpose and what do I desire to materialize in my life, right now?" The good news is, we can stop looking outside of ourselves for the answers because the answers are within us.

INTENT – is something that someone plans to do or achieve. We must consistently ask and answer these important questions for ourselves. We must *Know* that the answers are within us and will be revealed. At this level of empowerment, we will discover how profoundly powerful we are to fulfill our purpose and materialize our deepest goals and desires.

After identifying our goals and desires, we must visualize it and write a personal mission statement. Having a personal and professional vision and mission statement is critical to our next level of success. Once we are clear on our intent or at least have a concept of who we desire to be and what we desire to materialize, five things will happen:

1. We will instantly begin to access our Power Consciousness (to know that you can do a thing) to **attract and draw to ourselves more Health, Relationships, Advancement and Wealth.** As a result, we will feel a renewed sense of positive energy, confidence, peace, power, and focus.

2. We will **believe and have more confidence in our abilities to succeed in life.** As a result, the negative feelings of fear, doubt and insecurity will be replaced with power, courage, and knowing.

3. We no longer will allow for negative people, situations or circumstances to drain our energy or take us off focus. As a result, **life challenges will no longer have power or control over us.**

4. We will **feel a sense of hope and possibility** because we are now realizing that if we have desires in our hearts, then it must mean that we have the power to materialize those desires.

5. We will **send a powerful energy out into the universe.** Next, the universe will align the exact forces we need in order to fulfill our purposes and materialize our deepest goals and desires.

Implementing the Intention mechanism will motivate and empower us to discover a higher power within ourselves to fulfill our purpose and materialize our deepest goals and desires.

Again, having a personal and professional vision and mission statement is critical to achieving our next level of success. It must be in the forefront of our minds at all times.

Remember, anyone who has succeeded in life had to go through some form of healing and transformation process in order for them to have succeeded. Take it from one of the greatest inspirational classics of our time:

No one drifts into Success

"You don't have to be a futurist or a fortuneteller to be able to predict some one's future. You can do so by asking him or her one simple question, "What is your one definite purpose in life and what plans have you made to attain it?"

If you ask a hundred people that question, 98 of them will answer something like: "I'd like to make a good living and be as successful as I can." While the answer sounds good on the surface, if you dig a little deeper, you will find a drifter who will never get anything out of life except the leftovers of truly successful people. Those persons who have a definite purpose and a plan for attaining success.

To be Successful you must decide at this moment exactly what your goals are and lay out the steps by which you intend to reach it."

Think and Grow Rich, by Napoleon Hill
A Year of Growing Rich,
52 Steps to Achieving Life's Rewards

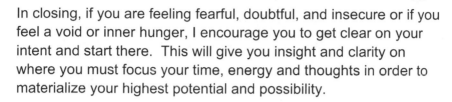

In closing, if you are feeling fearful, doubtful, and insecure or if you feel a void or inner hunger, I encourage you to get clear on your intent and start there. This will give you insight and clarity on where you must focus your time, energy and thoughts in order to materialize your highest potential and possibility.

The greatest thing that you can do for yourself and this world right now is to get clear on your intent. Constantly ask yourself the questions, "Who am I? What is my purpose? What do I desire? How should I overcome my life challenges to succeed?" Asking yourself these important questions will allow you to go beyond people, present situations or circumstances and begin operating at a higher level of Conscious Power. At this level of empowerment you will fulfill your purpose and materialize more love, joy, peace and prosperity into your life!

What Do You Think? Notes, Comments, Commitments:

_____

_____

_____

_____

_____

Health

Power Conscious Goal #1:

Ask yourself this question: Am I physically, mentally and emotionally strong enough within myself to overcome my life challenges to fulfill my purpose and achieve my deepest goals and desires?

If you answered, "yes" to the above question, then Bravo to you and keep up the great work that you are doing in the world.

If you answered "no" to the above question, do not feel bad, weak, frustrated or powerless. If your deepest intent is to materialize a healthier, stronger mind, body and spirit, then start now. Visualize and affirm with feeling and emotion this powerful affirmation as often as possible:

> ➢ **"Power Conscious, I intend to achieve a healthier, stronger mind, body and spirit. I Am Perfect Health – Every bone, muscle, tissue and cell of my body is filled with love and perfection. Therefore, I am eternally youthful, beautiful and in perfect health."**

At this level of Power Conscious thinking, we will naturally eliminate all self-destructive thoughts, beliefs and behaviors and replace them with **Self-Empowering thoughts, beliefs and behaviors.** In addition, we **will love and believe in ourselves more**. Mastering this concept will empower us to naturally develop a healthier stronger mind, body and spirit on a daily basis. At this level of physical, mental and spiritual health, we will **operate at our highest potential** to fulfill our purpose and materialize our deepest goals and desires. In addition, as we heal and transform our lives, we automatically **inspire other people** to heal and transform their lives.

What Do You Think? Notes, Comments, Commitments:

_____

_____

Have you forgiven yourself and people for any wrongdoing? Yes or No – If you answered "no" then ask yourself, "Is the un-forgiveness worth holding on to based on the negative impact it is making on your mind, body and spirit?"

_____

_____

_____

What are your negative addictions and what are you doing to prepare your mind, body and spirit to eliminate your dependency?

_____

_____

_____

What could be preventing you from loving, respecting and appreciating yourself unconditionally?

_____

_____

What do you need to "let go of and/or accept" in order to free yourself from bondage? (What belief, person, thing or behavior do you need to let go of in order have more energy?

_____

Relationships

Power Conscious Goal #2:

Ask yourself these questions: Am I getting along harmoniously in my relationships with the people in my personal and professional life? Am I attracting positive people who are intelligent, energized, motivated and joyous about life? Am I maintaining intimate relationships that make me feel happy, excited and alive?

If you answered, "yes" to the above questions, then Bravo to you and keep up the great work that you are doing in the world.

If you answered "no" to the above questions, do not feel disempowered, disconnected, alone or depressed. If your deepest intent is to create successful relationships with all people, personally and professionally, then start now. Visualize and affirm with feeling and emotion this powerful affirmation as often as possible:

> ➤ **"Power Conscious, I intend to create successful relationships with all people, both personally and professionally. I Only Have Loving Relationships With Everyone (Family, Friends, Enemies, The World) I love, respect and appreciate myself; therefore, I treat everyone with love and respect. I no longer feel the need to please people or understand why they do what they do. I accept**

people for who they are because I know who I Am. I am Powerful. I give Love. I give Love. I give Love."

At this level of Power Conscious thinking, we will heal and transform all negative relationships into **positive, loving, supportive relationships.** This will allow us to eliminate the negative drama from our relationships that tend to drain energy and take us off focus. Mastering this concept will **free us to be more joyous, energized and productive** in our lives. Furthermore, striving for successful relationships will allow us to **attract and connect with positive people** who are intelligent, energized, motivated and joyous about life. Lastly, creating successful relationships will empower us to work harmoniously with all people to **create more love, joy, peace and great riches in this world.**

What Do You Think? Notes, Comments, Commitments:

What do you need to heal and transform within yourself in order to produce loving, harmonious relationships with the people in your personal and professional life, now? **I need to heal & transform my:**

1. _____ Defensiveness
2. _____ Fears, doubts and insecurities
3. _____ Resentment, Un-forgiveness, Anger, Jealousy
4. _____ Negative judgments & conversations about people
5. _____ Co-dependence, neediness, and greediness
6. _____ Inability to have empathy for people
7. _____ Controlling and manipulating behaviors
8. _____ Internal battles, because "I am at war with myself"

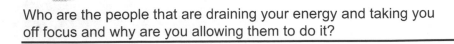
Who are the people that are draining your energy and taking you off focus and why are you allowing them to do it?

How are people able to make you feel insecure or dis-empowered and why are you allowing them to do it?

_____

_____

When are people able to manipulate and control you into doing things that are not in your spirit to do?

_____

_____

Whenever you observe yourself participating in any of these negative self-defeating behaviors, I encourage you to affirm your relationship affirmations as often as possible. This will empower you to refocus your time, energy and thoughts on creating relationships that are about Love, Joy, Peace and Harmony. You will be amazed at how profoundly powerful you are to transform your negative relationships into positive supportive relationships.

_____

_____

_____

What Do You Think? Notes, Comments, Commitments:

_____

_____

_____

_____

_____

Professional Advancement

Power Conscious Goal #3:

Ask yourself these questions: Am I getting great evaluations for the services I provide the people in my personal and professional life? Am I technically, mentally, emotionally, and physically prepared to advance professionally?

If you answered, "yes" to the above questions, then Bravo to you and keep up the great work that you are doing in the world.

If you answered "no," do not feel like a failure, discouraged, devalued, or hopeless. Moreover, do not make excuses and do not remain in denial about your weaknesses. This will only prolong your growth or destroy you in the end. If it is your deepest intent to advance professionally, then start now. Visualize and affirm with feeling and emotion this powerful affirmation as often as possible:

> **"Power Conscious, I intend to advance professionally." I Am A Professional – I am a professional because I know who I am, and I know that I can do all things with love that supports and strengthens me. Now, I operate at my fullest potential to give great service and achieve my personal and professional goals and desires.**

At this level of Power Conscious Thinking, we will develop our **critical thinking, self-management, professional behaviors, and technical skills**. In addition, we will **present and communicate ourselves in a professional manner** in order to get what we desire from this world, both personally and professionally. Mastering this concept will empower us to 1) present and communicate more effectively with all people 2) give great service, and 3) **put excellence into everything that we do**, personally and professionally. Furthermore, we will strengthen **our self-discipline, work ethic and leadership abilities**. All of which are required for professional advancement.

What Do You Think? Notes, Comments, Commitments:

_____

_____

On a scale of 1 – 5, what is your ability to effectively present and communicate your product or service to the world in order for this world to give you the LIFE you desire to live? How can you improve your presentation and communication skills?

_____

_____

What do you need to improve regarding yourself - in order to add more value and worth to your products or services? I need to improve on:

__ Patience with self and people
__ Ability to focus on a project until complete
__ Presentation and communication skills
__ Self-Management Skills
__ Interpersonal Skills (get along harmoniously with people)
__ My negative personality defaults
__ Ability to be more positive and optimistic

__ Increase energy level
__ Ability to say "no" to people and mean it.
__ Ability to become a stronger team player
__ Ability to see the bigger picture
__ Leadership Skills
__ Ability to give more of myself

Are you a Leader? What are your strengths and weaknesses as a Leader?

_____
_____
_____
_____

What Do You Think? Notes, Comments, Commitments:

_____
_____
_____
_____
_____
_____
_____
_____
_____
_____
_____
_____
_____
_____

Financial Wealth

Power Conscious Goal #4:

Ask yourself these questions: Am I attracting and materializing the level of financial wealth I truly desire and deserve? Am I mentally, emotionally, and spiritually prepared to receive the Financial Wealth I truly desire? Am I providing professional services at the level I desire to receive Financial Wealth?

If you answered, "yes" to the above questions, then Bravo to you and keep up the great work that you are doing in the world.

If you answered "no" to the above questions, do not feel like a failure with no self-worth or value. If it is your deepest intent to materialize financial wealth, then start now. Visualize and affirm with feeling and emotion this powerful affirmation as often as possible:

> ➢ **"Power Conscious, I intend to materialize financial wealth. I now connect with my inner power to grow and receive. I Am Powerful, Intelligent, Courageous and beautiful. I am the love, joy, peace and great riches I seek outside of myself. "**

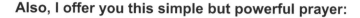

Also, I offer you this simple but powerful prayer:

"Oh, that You would bless me indeed, and enlarge my territory, that Your hand would be with me, and that You would keep me from evil."

**The Prayer of Jabez,
Breaking Through to the Blessed Life
by Bruce Wikinson**

At this level of Power Conscious Thinking, we will naturally **increase our self-esteem, energy level and our self-worth and value**. When we increase these elements within ourselves, we automatically develop a positive attitude and **put excellence into everything we do**. We **attract and draw** to ourselves more opportunities for **financial wealth and independence**. Moreover, at this level of empowerment, once we receive financial wealth, we will not sabotage our success, nor will we fear someone taking it away. Remember, when success is created from the inside out, it can never be destroyed or taken away from us.

We must also keep in mind, financial wealth is not the ultimate goal. Financial Wealth is an energy that allows us to bring into **physical manifestation the lifestyle we truly desire and deserve**. Remember, the more positive energy we give to the world, the more financial wealth and so much more we will receive.

What Do You Think? Notes, Comments, Commitments:

_____

_____

Right now, are you respecting money? Is this reflected in your daily spending and have you gone GREEN?

_____

_____

_____

Right now, are you giving thanks for what you have? If not, what can you give thanks for right now and build from there?

_____

_____

_____

What do you need to heal and transform within yourself in order to materialize financial wealth? I need to:

1. ____ Increase my self-esteem, self-worth and value
2. ____ Give more of myself, personally and professionally
3. ____ Believe there are enough resources for everyone
4. ____ Manage myself more effectively
5. ____ Listen to my intuition when making decisions
6. ____ Spend less than I earn
7. ____ Perform at a level that deserves higher pay
8. ____ Stop being so greedy, needy and ungrateful
9. ____ Stop looking to other people to make me successful
10. ____ Start being honest about my strengths and weaknesses
11. ____ Learn to say "no" to people and mean it

What can you do *right now* in order to create more financial wealth? The answers are always within you.

_____

_____

Do you know exactly how much income is coming in and how much income is going out? Are you spending your money appropriately?

Authentic Success

Power Conscious Goal #5:

Ask yourself these questions: Am I attracting and drawing to myself the level of love, joy, peace and great riches that I truly desire and deserve? Am I feeling great, looking great and producing great things in this world?

If you answered, "yes" to the above questions, then Bravo to you and keep up the great work that you are doing in the world.

If you answered "no" to the above questions, do not feel dis-empowered, low self-esteem, limited or hopeless. If it is your deepest intent to materialize authentic success, start now. Get a clear mental picture in your mind of you having more love, joy, peace and great riches. What does it look like and feel like? Next, visualize and affirm with feeling and emotion this powerful affirmation as often as possible:

> ➤ **"Power Conscious, I intend to materialize the love, joy, peace and great riches I truly desire and deserve."**

At this level of Power Conscious Thinking, we will **attract and draw to ourselves positive people, situations and circumstances that support us in fulfilling our purpose and achieving our goals and desires.** All of these will reflect the

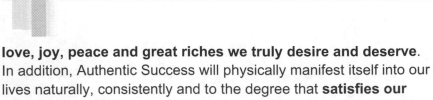
love, joy, peace and great riches we truly desire and deserve. In addition, Authentic Success will physically manifest itself into our lives naturally, consistently and to the degree that **satisfies our hearts and souls.** At this level of empowerment, we will not have to say one word because our energy will shine so brightly that others will see it and be attracted to it. Moreover, they will be inspired to materialize their heart's desires.

Always remember, we are the love, joy, peace and prosperity that we seek outside of ourselves. We must spend time discovering these elements within ourselves. They are there. We must meditate, affirm, visualize and re-direct our energy on the love, joy, peace and great riches we desire to achieve. When it is revealed and discovered from within, ultimately it will be materialized externally. Practicing this concept will always yield powerful results. This is a universal law. Practice!

What Do You Think? Notes, Comments, Commitments:

_____

_____

_____

What or who do you need to stop allowing to have power and control over you, in order for you to materialize more love, joy, peace and great riches in your life?

_____

_____

_____

_____

_____

_____

_____

Questions and Answers:

1. Why are we not clear on who we desire to be and what we desire to create? Why don't we know our deepest intent? We are too consumed by the world around us. It is difficult to take time out for "self" outside our tribe or culture. However, the world is slowly but surely realizing that quiet "self" time is essential to our personal growth and development. Moreover, I believe that this process is a critical component to our healing and transforming this world. What do you think?

2. What if we are crystal clear on our goals and desires but things are not materializing in the way that we envisioned? It could be because our personal vision does not match up with our higher power's vision. Or it may mean that we have more to learn, like patience, poise (peace and power) and process. Not to mention, we may need to learn how to treat people better. Seek a realization from within yourself. The answer is there. What do you think?

3. What if you just don't have the time to get clear on your intent or for your personal and professional development? Why can't we find the time? We find time for everything and everyone else. If we cannot find the time to get clear on our goals and desires, then we cannot get angry or frustrated when we are not getting what we desire. When our development and desires become important enough, we will find the time to sit-down in a seat and ask ourselves the questions, "Who do I desire to be and what do I desire to materialize in my life, right now?" The answers will come because they are already waiting for us to bring them into physical manifestation. This will give us the motivation we really need to move our lives to the next of level success. What do you think?

4. What if you are crystal clear on what you truly desire, but you just don't believe that it is possible in two million years? Affirm, I Am Powerful Enough over and over again. This will allow us to rise above our fears, doubts or insecurities, and encourage us to ACT. It will empower us to keep putting one-foot-in-front-of-the-other until we have succeeded. This is how we will discover how powerful we are to materialize our deepest desires, despite our fears, doubts and insecurities. What do you think?

5. What if your intent goes completely against your tribe or culture's intent for you? I will say to you directly: Make a decision now to move on the intent that you truly believe will allow you to fulfill your purpose and materialize your deepest desires, and don't look back. This is if you truly desire to be happy and successful in your life. Otherwise, you will blame the tribe or culture if you are not feeling happy or satisfied with your life. What do you think?

5 Power Conscious Decisions For Success Now

1. I decide now to look **beyond negative appearances and seek the truth.** Mastering this concept will empower me to discover how profoundly powerful I am to transform negative appearances into positive truths.

2. I decide now to **relax and be patient with myself and people**, while at the same time, doing what must be done in order to materialize my deepest goals and desires. Mastering this concept will empower me to **re-energize, think more clearly and take the necessary action steps** required in order to achieve my daily objectives.

3. I decide now to **listen to my intuition and follow through** on what it tells me to do. Mastering this concept will allow me to tap into a higher level of intelligence in order to materialize my deepest goals and desires.

4. I decide now to **take back the power** that I have given to negative people, situations or circumstances. Mastering this concept will allow me to re-focus my time, energy and thoughts on materializing my highest potential and possibility. I now realize that I have enough power to fulfill my purpose and create a great life.

5. I decide now **to take risks and never give up** on discovering how profoundly powerful I am to set goals and do what must be done in order to bring those goals into physical manifestation. I am powerful enough. I am Powerful enough to **make effective decisions that support me in materializing my deepest goals and desires**.

Decide Now

Ask yourself these questions, "Have I made a conscious decision to fulfill my purpose and achieve my goals and desires, no matter what? Have I made a conscious decision to overcome life challenges with grace to materialize the love, joy, peace and great riches I desire?

Once we are clear on our intent to materialize specific goals and desires, now it is time to make a definite decision to succeed. Definiteness of decision is a requirement for Success, because it gives us the confidence, direction, and focus needed to ACT and produce powerful results.

When we make a definite decision to succeed, this does not mean an over night success. We will have setbacks, people may not support our decisions, and we will face challenges along the way. However, making a definite decision to succeed will empower us to do 5 things:

Making A Definite Decision

1. It will empower us to **develop the mindset to keep moving forward** in life regardless of negative people, setbacks and challenges we may face along the way.

2. It will empower us to access an energy within us that lets the world know that we are serious about what we have decided.

3. It will empower us to **send a powerful energy out into the universe** that aligns the exact forces that we need in order

to succeed in the accomplishments of our goals and desires.

4. It will help us to eliminate negative conversations and **refocus on positive conversations that support our decision to succeed.**

5. This process will allow us to eliminate indecision, procrastination, frustration and uncertainty. In addition, **it will empower us to attract and draw to ourselves - positive people, situations and circumstances that will assist in our success.**

After making a definite decision to succeed, we must trust and believe that the universe will align the exact forces that we need in order to yield powerful results. In addition, we must also trust and have faith that we are powerful enough to follow through on our decision to succeed.

We must remember, only we can create our success and only we can block our success. If our decision to succeed is stronger than our indecisiveness, we will succeed regardless of life challenges. Please do not procrastinate on internalizing this powerful concept.

Think and Grow Rich
"The Mastery of Procrastination"
Analysis of several hundred people who had accumulated fortunes well beyond the million-dollar mark disclosed the fact that every one of them had the habit of reaching decisions promptly, and of changing these decisions slowly, if and when they were changed. People who failed to accumulate money, without exception, have the habit of reaching a decision, if at all, very slowly, and of changing these decisions quickly and often.

The majority of people who fail to accumulate money sufficient for their needs are, generally, easily influenced by the opinion of others. They permit the newspapers and the gossiping neighbors to do their thinking for them. Opinions are the cheapest commodities on earth. Everyone has a flock of opinions ready to be wished upon anyone who will accept them. If you are influenced by opinions when you reach a decision, you will not succeed in any undertaking, much less in that of transmuting your own desire into money. If you are influenced by the opinions of others, you will have no desire of your own.

Close friends and relatives, while not meaning to do so, often handicap one through "opinions" and sometimes through ridicule, which is meant to be humorous. Thousands of men and women carry inferiority complexes with them all through life, because some well-meaning but ignorant person destroyed their confidence through "opinions" or ridicule.

You have a brain and mind of your own. Use it, and reach your own decision. If you need facts or information from other people to enable you to reach decisions, as you probably will in many instances, acquire these facts or secure the information you need quietly, without disclosing your purpose.

Let one of your first decisions be to keep a closed mouth and open ears and eyes. As a reminder to yourself to follow this advice, it will be helpful if you copy the following epigram in large letters and place it where you will see it daily: **"Tell the world what you intend to do, but first show it."** This is the equivalent of saying that "Deeds, and not words, are what counts most."

**Think And Grow Rich, The Inspirational Classic
By Napoleon Hill**

If it is our deepest intent to succeed in life, then we must make a conscious decision to materialize this goal. A definite decision will empower us to overcome procrastination, setbacks, indecision and frustration. In addition, it will allow us to conquer our fears, doubts and insecurities to create the life we desire to live. What do you think?

What Do You Think? Notes, Comments, Commitments:

_____

_____

_____

_____

_____

_____

_____

_____

_____

_____

_____

_____

Seek The Truth

Decision #1:

We must Decide now to **Look Beyond the negative appearances and seek the truth**. Looking beyond negative appearances and seeking the truth will empower us to "judge not according to appearances but judge positive judgments."

Mastering this concept will empower us to stop getting caught-up in negative appearances and re-focus on seeing positive truths. One truth is that all is in divine order. Another truth is that we are powerful beyond measure. And yet another truth is that all appearances are not real. At this level of power conscious thinking, negative appearances will melt away and positive truths will be revealed.

The next time that you are faced with a negative appearance and you start to feel fearful, overwhelmed or depressed, (this could be a negative person, situation or circumstance), I encourage you to affirm this powerful affirmation:

➢ **I decide now to look beyond negative appearances and seek the truth. Mastering this concept will empower me to discover how profoundly powerful I am to transform negative appearances into positive truths.**

What Do You Think? Notes, Comments, Commitments:

_____

_____

_____

Relax and Be Patient

Decision #2:

Decide now to **Relax and be patient with yourself and people** as you go through the process of fulfilling your purpose and materializing your goals and desires.

We must learn to relax and be patient, while at the same time, we must **take the necessary action steps** required fulfill our purpose and to materialize our goals and desires. Relaxing and being patient will empower us to **feel energized and confident** about materializing success, verses feeling discouraged and stressed. Also, relaxing and being patient will allow for **our lives to unfold in divine order.** At this level of conscious awareness, all that is ours by divine right will physically materialize itself in divine order. Be still and "know", relax and be patient.

The next time you start to feel frustrated, angry, overwhelmed, impatient, stressed-out or if you start to feel consumed by the world around you, I encourage you to affirm this powerful affirmation within yourself:

> ➤ **I decide now to relax and be patient with myself and people, while at the same time, doing what must be done in order to fulfill our purpose and materialize my deepest goals and desires. Mastering this concept will empower me to re-energize, think more clearly and take the necessary action steps required in order to achieve my daily objectives.**

What Do You Think?

Listen to Your Intuition
Decision #3:

Decide now to **listen to your intuition and follow through** on what it tells you to do. This will allow you to tap into a higher level of intelligence in order to fulfill your purpose and materialize your deepest goals and desires.

Our intuition is that **inner VOICE** that speaks to us directly. It may say, "Be patient because there is a greater opportunity for advancement up the road." Intuition might say, "Listen to this person because they have your best interest in mind" or "don't listen to this person because they do not have your best interest in mind." Our intuition might say, "Get out of this environment because something negative is about to happen" or "Stay in this environment because there is something greater to be gained."

If it is our deepest intent to succeed in life, then we must get in the habit of listening to our intuition. Our intuition is **our highest level of divine intelligence.** It will empower us to **make effective decisions that support our true purpose and ultimate goals and desires.** In addition, it will help us to avoid future mistakes, setbacks and disappointments. Lastly, when our intuition speaks, we must **trust and believe that we have the courage to follow-through on what our intuition is telling us to do**. And do it, no questions asked. Our intuition is powerful.

The next time you observe yourself feeling that something is not quite right, or if you feel indecisive or unsure of what you should do regarding a specific person or situation, I encourage you to be still and affirm the following affirmation to yourself.

> **I now decide to listen to my intuition and follow through on what it tells me to do. Mastering this concept will allow me to tap into a higher level of intelligence in order to discover solutions, achieve my purpose and materialize my deepest goals and desires.**

These powerful words will allow you to do two things, 1) access a higher level of divine intelligence and 2) develop the courage to do what it tells you to do.

What Do You Think? Notes, Comments, Commitments:

_____

_____

_____

_____

_____

_____

_____

Take Back the Power

Decision #4:

Decide now, we must **take back the power** that we have given to negative people, situations and circumstances and refocus that energy on **being who we desire to be and creating what we desire to create in our life.**

Mastering this concept will empower us to take back the power we have given to negativity and refocus that time, energy and thought on creating more health, relationships, advancement and wealth.

The next time you observe yourself losing power or feeling dis-empowered, discouraged, defeated or drained of your energy, I encourage you to affirm the following affirmation:

> ➤ I decide now to **take back the power** that I have given to negative people, situations or circumstances. Mastering this concept will allow me to re-focus my time, energy and thoughts on materializing my highest potential and possibility. I now realize that I have the power enough to fulfill my purpose and create a great life.

What does taking back our power mean? Ultimately, the things or people that use to dis-empower or dis-encourage us will no longer have power or control over us. Moreover, we are freed-up to fulfill our purpose and materialize our deepest goals and desire in this world. This is one of the greatest feelings that any one can have.

What Do You Think?

_____

Take Risks

Decision #5:

Decide now, we must **take risks and never give up on discovering** how profoundly powerful we are to set goals and do what must be done in order to bring those goals into physical manifestation.

In other words, we must get in the habit of **successfully completing what we start.** When we make a decision to achieve a specific goal, then we must not allow for outside influences to discourage or block our success. When we make a decision to succeed in life and we meet with temporary defeat, we must not allow it to dis-empower us from continuing to **move forward, no matter what.**

Mastering this concept will empower us to take risks and never give up on discovering how profoundly powerful we are to set goals and do what must be done in order to bring those goals into physical manifestation.

The next time you observe yourself feeling fear, doubt or insecure or the next time you want to give-up because of negative influences, such as negative people, situations or circumstances; I encourage you to affirm this powerful affirmation:

> ➢ **I now decide to take risks and never give up on discovering how profoundly powerful I am to set goals and do what must be done in order to bring those goals into physical manifestation. I am powerful enough. I am Powerful enough. I am Powerful enough to make effective decisions that support me in materializing my deepest goals and desires.**

What Do You Think?

Assignment

Here are some personal statements of people who made a decision, and have gotten life changing results. Check the items that speak to you directly and review them often when you start to feel indecisive or unsure of yourself.

1. _____ I made a conscious decision to give up the victim role. It no longer works. This is teaching me how to stand up for myself. I am learning how to tell people "no" and mean it. Plus, I do not feel guilty or bad for saying, "no". This has changed my life because now I have more time and energy to create the life I truly desire.

2. _____ I made a decision to stop worrying and re-focus that energy on creating the life "I say" is important to me. This has allowed me to dramatically decrease my stress level and become more focused. Now, I am far happier and productive in my daily life.

3. _____ I made a decision to stop looking back over my past mistakes and setbacks. It feels like a big burden has been lifted off my shoulders. Making the decision to let-go-of-my-past has freed me up to think more clearly about what I have the potential to create for myself, from this point forward.

4. _____ I decided to stop allowing negative people to have power and control over me. This was, and still is, one of the hardest things I have done in my life. But, it has brought me the greatest peace and harmony. Now I feel like I am powerful enough to do anything I truly desire to do.

5. _____ I decided to forgive myself for bad things I have done in the past. This decision has healed and transformed my life. I am so much happier and excited about my life. Even in challenging times, I am still motivated and determined to succeed.

6. _____ I decided to leave my relationship that was no longer working. Even though we are still in the same household, I am at peace and I have clarity. This has allowed me to think more clearly and realistically about my life. It has forced me to develop a stronger, more powerful relationship with myself. This has given me the inner strength I needed to move my life forward.

7. _____ I decided to start my own company; no one supported me and everyone told me I was crazy. This year we are celebrating our 12th year in business. It was not always easy. However, I am so grateful that I listened to my intuition, because I am happier than I ever thought possible.

8. _____ I decided that if I did not materialize the life I envisioned for myself, it would not be the end of the world. I will still give 110% to my goals, but not in a self-destructive manner. This has allowed me to be at peace and live more in the present. I also realized I no longer have to compete with other people. This has made me feel more balanced and secure within myself.

9. _____ I decided to stop allowing my fears, doubts and insecurities blocking me from "doing what must be done" in order to materialize my goals and desires. This has allowed me to truly understand what it means to surrender

to my higher power. When I find myself procrastinating or making excuses, I affirm: "I am Powerful enough to do this." This helps me to re-focus myself and keep moving forward.

10. _____ I made a decision to stop making excuses for not stepping-up to the plate and delivering. Now, when I miss a deadline or forget to take out the trash, I do not beat myself up. I just apologize and re-commit myself to doing better. Plus, this concept is healing and transforming my relationships with the people in my life.

Questions and Answers

1. What should you do if you have so many options, you just cannot make a decision on 3 or 4 things? Please realize it is time to grow-up and make some concrete decisions before you don't have a choice any longer. If you need some help making a decision, decide on a few things that will empower you the most. What do you think?

2. What if you are clear on your desires and you have made a decision to succeed, but you keep failing over and over again? Remember Thomas Edison had 10,000 failures before he succeeded in inventing the incandescent light. If you are serious about creating greatness in your life, take off your watch and don't feel like a failure until after your 10,000th attempt at creating greatness. What do you think?

3. What if you have decided to succeed, but you keep going back on your decision, for one reason or another? This is a major part of success. If you are truly serious about succeeding, stop worrying, you will succeed. But, if you are

not serious about succeeding and have no real intent on following through on your decisions, then you are only kidding yourself. Moreover, you are wasting energy that could be focused on discovering how powerful you are to create greatness and serve humanity. What do you think?

4. What if you can't make a decision because you are waiting for him or her to make up their mind about what they want to do? Please realize, your decision to succeed in life has nothing to do with what anyone else decides. Make decisions based on what is in your heart to do. And when that person makes a decision about what they are going to do, if it is in alignment with your decisions, great. If it is not, even greater because then you will not have that uncertainty pulling on you. Furthermore, you will save yourself time, energy and thought, that can be refocused on creating the life you ultimately desire to live. What do you think?

5. What should I do when I find myself wavering on my decisions to succeed? Keep Deciding Now to Succeed until you Succeed. Practicing your affirmations will empower you to keep moving forward. What do you think?

5 Power Conscious Realizations For Action

Moving from an Understanding to Action

PC Realization for Action #1:

I now realize that I must **Operate At My Highest Potential** on a daily basis in order to provide great service and put excellence into accomplishing my goals and desires.

PC Realization for Action #2

I now realize that I must **Think Powerfully** in order to overcome my life challenges to Succeed in life.

PC Realization for Action #3

I now realize that I must **Believe and have Confidence** in my ability to "do what must be done" in order to successfully complete my daily objectives.

PC Realization for Action #4

I now realize that I must **Make Effective Decisions** on a daily basis that will support the achievement of my deepest goals and desires.

PC Realization for Action #5

I now realize that I must **Take Action Now** if my deepest intent is to fulfill my purpose and materialize my personal and professional goals and desires.

At this level of Power Conscious thinking, ultimately you will be motivated to **discover the power within, to "Do What Must Be Done"** in order to materialize your goals and desires.

Realization - Moving from an Understanding to Action

Do you UNDERSTAND the basic mental, emotional, spiritual and physical processes that must take place before YOU CAN effectively fulfill your purpose and MATERIALIZE your goals and desires? Do you know what you need to heal and transform within yourself, before you can effectively take your life to the next level of Success?

Realization - to know, understand and accept. Now that we are clear on our intent and have made a decision to succeed, when life is not moving in divine order or when we keep meeting the temporary defeat, we should ask ourselves these questions: What is it that I need to realize within myself, in order to materialize success, now? What do I need to realize from within myself In order to materialize more Health, Relationships, Professional Advancement and Financial Wealth?

Consistently asking ourselves these questions will allow us to realize what we need to heal and transform within ourselves in order to bring about positive results that lead to success. We may need to change our thinking about a particular person or situation, from negative to positive. It may mean that we need to take responsibility for something or someone even though we do not want to. It may mean we need to come out of denial and realize a higher truth about ourselves. Once we realize what we need to heal and transform within ourselves and address the issues, the universe will assist in our success. At this point, authentic success will be the result. Our external successes will begin to match-up with our internal successes. This is a universal law. In other words, before we can effectively materialize external success, we

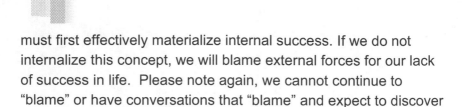

must first effectively materialize internal success. If we do not internalize this concept, we will blame external forces for our lack of success in life. Please note again, we cannot continue to "blame" or have conversations that "blame" and expect to discover solutions and produce positive results.

One of the greatest things that we can do right now to influence external success is to take responsibility for our part in the whole of success. We can do this by realizing specifically what we need to heal and transform within ourselves in order to discover positive solutions and produce powerful results in our lives.

How do we know if we need to come to a higher realization before we can materialize our next level of success?

    a. Whenever life is not moving in divine order or when things are not moving fast enough, it means we need to seek a higher realization.

    b. When we keep meeting with the same defeat, setback, negative person, addiction, etc., over and over, it means we need to seek a higher realization.

    c. When we observe ourselves saying one thing and doing another, and then cannot understand why we keep meeting with temporary defeat, it means we need to seek a higher realization.

    d. When we keep having the same argument in our relationships with people, it means we need to come to a higher realization about the root of the problem and not just the top surface issues.

Practicing this concept will motivate and empower us to do the inner work required for personal success. Moreover, realizing what we need to heal and transform within ourselves to succeed in the external world will allow us to:

1. **Take the focus off the external world and place it on the internal world**. Remember, it has been concluded that we must first create internal success before materializing external success, (our internal world is a reflection of our external world.) Change the internal world and the external world will change automatically. Practicing this concept will empower us to take responsibility for our destiny in life.

2. Develop the mindset and critical thinking skills required for us to **come up with solutions for our life challenges.** This concept will empower us to overcome life challenges in order to succeed in life.

3. Empower ourselves to discover the power within to **"do what must be done,"** and "master what needs to be mastered," in order to succeed in the external world.

At this level of empowerment, we will realize the Power of the Human spirit to transform negative results and failures in to Positive Results and Successes.

Operate At My Highest Potential

Realization for Action #1:

I now realize that I must Operate At My Highest Potential on a daily basis in order to provide great service and put excellence into accomplishing my goals and desires.

Operating at our highest potential simply means to consistently focus and **re-focus our time, energy and thoughts on doing what must be done in order to fulfill our purpose and materialize our deepest goals and desire**. And we must do it with love and grace. When we are operating at our highest potential, we will approach every task in a powerful manner. Every thought will be a powerful thought and every action will be a powerful action.

Each day we will **grow stronger and become more powerful within ourselves**. Practicing this concept will empower us to become more focused and productive in our daily lives.

What Do You Think? Notes, Comments, Commitments:

Where do I need to step-up in my personal and professional life?

_____

_____

_____

Think Powerfully

Realization for Action #2:

I now realize that I must Think Powerfully in order to overcome life challenges to Succeed in life.

To Think Powerfully simply means to think, **"I Am Powerful, Intelligent, Courageous and Beautiful."** To think powerfully also means to eliminate all limited, negative thoughts, beliefs and concepts and re-focus on powerful thoughts, beliefs and concepts. Practicing this concept will empower us to think at a higher level of intelligence in order to **1) clarify our highest vision, 2) develop and implement a plan of action, 3) find solutions to challenges and 4) succeed in the accomplishment of our deepest goals and desires.**

What Do You Think? Notes, Comments, Commitments:

_____

_____

What areas of my life do I need to think more powerfully about myself?

_____

_____

What negative thoughts do I need to replace with powerful thoughts?

_____

_____

_____

_____

Believe and have Confidence

Realization for Action #3:

I now realize that I must Believe and have Confidence in my ability to "do what must be done" in order to successfully complete my daily objectives.

Believing and having confidence simply means to **be who we desire to be and create what we desire to create** in this world, regardless of negative people, situations or circumstances. It also means to eliminate all fears, doubts and insecurities from our consciousness and **surrender to a higher power** within ourselves in order to succeed in life. At this level of empowerment, we will develop our belief and confidence in our ability to materialize ANYTHING that we put our minds towards achieving. If we put our minds to healing and transforming our lives, then we will succeed. If we put our minds to materialize more health, successful relationships, professional advancement or financial wealth, then we will succeed. This is a universal law.

What Do You Think? Notes, Comments, Commitments:

_____

_____

What is my **"Do what Must Be Done"** that I have been procrastinating on for one reason or another? Would "just doing it," allow me to take my life to the next level of Success?

_____

_____

Make Effective Decisions

Realization for Action #4:

I now realize that I must Make Effective Decisions on a daily basis that will support the achievement of my deepest goals and desires.

Making a series of Good Decisions will allow us to dramatically increase our success rate and eliminate stress, confusion and indecision. In addition, it places us in a stronger position to take full advantage of life's greatest opportunities for personal and professional advancement.

What Do You Think? Notes, Comments, Commitments:

_____
_____
_____
_____

What are some areas in my life where I need to start making better decisions to support my deepest goals and desires?

_____
_____
_____
_____
_____
_____

Take Action Now

Realization for Action #5

I now realize that I must Take Action Now if my deepest intent is to fulfill my purpose and materialize my personal and professional goals and desires.

If it is our deepest intent to succeed in life, then we must **take consistent action towards fulfilling our purpose and materializing our deepest goals and desires.** After meditating, visualizing and affirming our deepest goals and desires, we must take the necessary action steps required to bring those goals and desires into physical manifestation. Period!

What Do You Think? Notes, Comments, Commitments:

_____

_____

What are some consistent action steps that I can take that would move me closer to my goals and desires?

_____

_____

_____

_____

_____

_____

Assignment

Here are some realizations that have healed and transformed lives in major ways. Check the ones that speak to you directly.

1. ____ I realized that I must stop living in a fantasy world before I can influence external success. This has allowed me to come out of denial and face the reality of my life. It also is helping me to stop playing mental games with myself and other people and refocus on creating the life I have the potential to live.

2. ____ I realized that I must stop blaming everyone else for the reasons that I do not love, respect and appreciate myself. This has allowed me to re-focus on learning to really love, respect and appreciate myself more, and develop stronger, more meaningful relationships with the people in my life.

3. ____ I realized that I have to let some people go before I can effectively materialize the external success I truly desire and deserve. This has freed me up to have more time and energy to materialize the life I truly desire and deserve.

4. ____ I realized that I must stop getting intoxicated before I will materialize external success and happiness. This has empowered me to face my addictions that are destroying my life and the lives of the people around me. I now realize that I must refocus that time and energy on creating the life I truly desire and deserve.

5. ____I realized that I must stop beating myself up because there is no value or worth in doing it. This has empowered me to be more forgiving of myself and others. In addition, it has allowed me to build a stronger relationship with myself and others.

6. ____ I realized that I can no longer get caught up in negative drama if I intend to materialize a great life for myself. Also, I must let go of everyone else's drama. This means that I must no longer participate in negative drama on any level, if I intend to materialize the great life I desire to live.

7. ____ I realized that I am my own worst enemy and I am at war with myself. Moreover, if I am at war with myself, then I will be at war with the people in my life. Realizing this has allowed me to end the war with myself and end the war I had going on with other people.

8. ____ I realized that I was blaming my family for me not being able to be all that I can be. Coming to this realization has empowered me to create a new life for myself. This has given me a renewed sense of power, peace and purpose.

9. ____ I realized that I have been putting the cart before the horse. Meaning, I have been seeking love, joy, peace and great riches outside of myself, before I have discovered these traits within myself. This knowledge has empowered me to put my life into perspective and set some priorities. In addition, it has empowered me to live a more balanced and peaceful life regardless of life challenges.

Questions and Answers

1. What if you intellectually understand the realization but you don't have the energy to act upon it? If we do not have the energy to reinforce our realizations through our actions, it is usually because we are allowing something or someone to drain our energy. With this understanding, we must learn to effectively manage our energy if our deepest intent is to succeed in life. What do you think?

2. What if you avoid coming to any realizations because it would mean that your entire life would have to change and you are just not ready?
   - First, we do not have a realization unless we are ready and it is time. Remember, change is challenging. However, the benefit of change is healing and transformational and will materialize great results.
   - Second, you may want to stop saying, "I am not ready. I am not ready." And replace it with, "I am ready. I am ready." Remember, words are very powerful and will manifest themselves when we affirm them. "I am powerful. I am ready for change."
   - Third, do not fear change because the universe is always working with you to move your life forward. Trust, have faith and believe in a higher power. What do you think?

3. What if the people with whom you associate have a "whatever" attitude about life and this encourages you to have a "whatever" attitude about life? I would say, back away slowly from such people. If you need some motivation, remember, people with a "whatever" attitude will

draw "whatever"/negative results. People with a positive attitude draw to themselves positive, successful results. Which do you truly desire to attract and draw to yourself, negative "whatever" results or positive successful results? What do you think?

4. "What if things are failing because of "them"... the negative people? I am doing all that I can do." Stop playing the victim because it no longer works; discover a power within you and take the focus off the external world and place it on the internal world. This will allow you to influence successful results. What do you think?

5. What is the greatest realization that a person can come to? One of the greatest realizations that we can come to right now is, "I Am Powerful Enough and I can fulfill my purpose and I can materialize my deepest goals and desires." To realize right now that we have everything that we need to succeed in life and to start acting on that possibility is the greatest realization we can come to for this planet and ourselves. What do you think?

What Do You Think? Notes, Comments, Commitments:

_____

_____

_____

_____

_____

_____

_____

_____

5 Power Conscious Attitudes For Success Now

1. I can and **I will forgive myself and forgive other people** for any wrongdoings. This will allow me to be open and receptive to Healing and Transforming my life beyond my wildest dreams. I Give Thanks!

2. I can and **I will believe and have confidence in my ability** to operate at my highest potential in order to create love, joy, peace and great riches on this earth. I Give Thanks!

3. I can and **I will react and respond to life powerfully**, regardless of what life puts before me. This will empower me to react and respond to life powerfully in order to create the great life I truly desire and deserve. Not just for myself, but for all the people on this planet. I Give Thanks!

4. I can and I will **stop allowing negative people, situations and circumstances to drain my energy and take me off focus. I will re-focus that energy on realizing my highest potential** to materialize my deepest goals and desires. I Give Thanks!

5. I can and **I will attract into my life positive people, situations and circumstances** that reflect and support my deepest goals and desires. In addition, I can and I will attract the love, joy, peace and great riches I truly desire and deserve. I Give Thanks!

I Can! I Will! It Is Done! I Give Thanks!

A Power Conscious Attitude

Your Attitude today determines your success tomorrow!
Keith Harrell, Attitude Is Everything

Do you have a positive attitude or a negative attitude about the way in which your life is unfolding? What does your inner conversation say about who you desire to be and what you desire to materialize? Is it positive or negative? In other words, are you optimistic about the possibilities of LIFE and your potential to fulfill your purpose and materialize your deepest goals and desires?

You must be the observer of yourself to answer these questions. No one else can tell you if you have a positive or negative attitude. Ask yourself the following questions to determine if you have a positive attitude or a negative attitude.

1. How am I feeling inside myself right now? Positive or Negative
2. How am I reacting and responding to what is unfolding in my life? Positive or Negative
3. How are the people in my life reacting and responding to me? Positively or Negatively
4. How do I feel about my current situations and circumstances and am I managing them effectively? (Health, Relationships, Career, Finances as a whole of success) Positive or Negative
5. What level of confidence do I have that I will fulfill my purpose and materializing my deepest goals and desires? Positive or Negative

When we have a negative attitude, we get negative results. When we have a positive attitude, we get positive results. If it is our deepest intent to succeed in life, then we must develop and maintain a positive attitude about the above questions. This is regardless of negative people, situations or circumstances. Right now, we must affirm with power and authority: "I can, I will, It is done, I Give Thanks," as often as possible. This will empower us to master a positive attitude. When we have a positive attitude, regardless of life challenges, we will yield positive results.

Remember, this is a universal law. Developing a positive attitude will allow us to:

1. **Overcome life challenges in a powerful manner** in order to fulfill our purpose and materialize our deepest desires.

2. **Manage and control the quality of our thoughts** leading to what we do and how we react and respond to life.

3. Put poise, peace and power into **executing our daily tasks and objectives with excellence.**

4. **Attract and draw to ourselves positive people, situations and circumstances** that support our life mission.

5. And lastly, a positive attitude empowers us to **feel better, look better and do better**, thereby improving the overall quality of our Health, Relationships, Career and Finances.

The great part about our attitude is that if it's negative, we can make it positive. Each of us has the power to exercise a positive attitude over a negative attitude.

At this level of empowerment, we will go on to improve the overall quality of our lives. In addition, we will go on to fulfill our purpose and to materialize our ultimate personal and professional goals and desires. In addition, we will attract and draw to ourselves more love, joy, peace and prosperity into our lives.

What Do You Think? Notes, Comments, Commitments:

_____

_____

_____

_____

_____

_____

_____

_____

_____

_____

_____

_____

_____

I Can! I Will! It is Done! I Give Thanks!

Forgive

Power Conscious Attitude #1:

Ask yourself this question, "Who do I need to forgive in order to expand my consciousness to receive more love, joy, peace and great riches into my life?" (I need to forgive_____.)
Now, develop a "power conscious attitude" by affirming:

> ➢ **I can and I will forgive myself and forgive other people for any wrongdoings. This will allow me to be open and receptive to Healing and Transforming my life beyond my wildest dreams. I Give Thanks!**

If it is our deepest intent to succeed in life, then we must forgive ourselves and other people for any wrongdoings. In addition, **we must re-focus that energy on fulfilling our purpose and materializing our deepest goals and desires.** Remember, one of the most powerful things that we can do to succeed in life, is to forgive. Why? Un-forgiveness is an energy drainer that blocks us from being open and receptive to receive love or success. When we are willing to forgive and **get the lesson,** we expand our consciousness to attract and receive greater love, joy, peace and great riches into our lives.

What Do You Think? Notes, Comments, Commitments:

_____

_____

_____

I Can! I Will! It is Done! I Give Thanks!

Believe In My Highest Potential & Possibility

Power Conscious Attitude #2:

Ask yourself this question, "Today, what is my highest Potential and Possibility? (It is possible for me to _____.) Now, develop a "power conscious attitude" in order to believe and have confidence in your ability to succeed by affirming:

> ➤ **I can and I will believe and have confidence in my ability to operate at my highest potential in order to create love, joy, peace and great riches on this earth. I Give Thanks!**

Oprah Winfrey said, "You do not become what you want or what you dream, you become what you believe inside of yourself." If it is our deepest intent to succeed in life, then we must believe and have confidence in our highest potential to be who we desire to be and create what we desire to create, while mastering our God-given gifts and talents. Moreover, we must be able to accept constructive criticism and give constructive criticism with love, compassion and grace. Practicing this attitude will empower us to master what needs to be mastered in order reach our highest potential and possibility in this life time.

What Do You Think? Notes, Comments, Commitments:

_____

_____

_____

I Can! I Will! It is Done! I Give Thanks!

React & Respond to Life Powerfully

Power Conscious Attitude #3:

Ask yourself this question, "What challenge am I faced with that is draining my energy and blocking me from materializing my next level of success?" (I am challenged by _____.) Now, develop a "power conscious attitude" to regain your power and affirm:

> ➤ **I can and I will react and respond to life powerfully, regardless of what life puts before me. This will empower me to overcome my life challenges in order to create the great life I truly desire and deserve. Not just for myself, but for all the people on this planet. I Give Thanks!**

If it is our deepest desire to succeed in life, then regardless of what life gives us, good or bad, **we must react and respond to life powerfully**. Please realize, at every level of success, there will be life challenges that we will have to overcome. **This is what makes us stronger**. Although we may not be responsible for the life challenges that come to us, we are responsible for our reaction and response to them. Remember, the blessing in every life challenge is the realization that we are powerful beyond measure. Adopting this attitude will empower us to **use all life challenges as opportunities to discover how profoundly powerful we are to create more love, joy, peace and great riches in this world.**

What Do You Think? Notes, Comments, Commitments:

_____

I Can! I Will! It is Done! I Give Thanks!

Re-Energize & Re-Focus
Power Conscious Attitude #4:

Ask yourself this question, "Right now, what is draining my energy and taking me off focus?" (I am tired and unfocused because _____.) Now let's get our energy and focus back by affirming this powerful affirmation:

> ➢ **I can and I will stop allowing negative people, situations and circumstances to drain my energy and take me off focus. I will re-focus that energy on realizing my highest potential and possibility to materialize my deepest goals and desires. I Give Thanks!**

Hear this loud and clear, if it is our deepest intent to fulfill our purpose and materialize our heart's desires then we must NOT allow negativity (in any form) to drain our energy and take us off focus. Period! Remember, we have the power within us to choose not to allow negativity to drain our energy and take us off focus. Internalizing this attitude will empower us to stop allowing negativity (in any form) to drain our energy and take us off focus. At this level of empowerment, we will have the energy and focus required to realize our highest potential and possibility.

What Do You Think? Notes, Comments, Commitments:

I Can! I Will! It is Done! I Give Thanks!

Think Powerfully

Power Conscious Attitude #5:

Ask yourself this question, "Who do I desire to be and what do I desire to create with the rest of my life?" (I desire _____.) Now, develop a "positive attitude" in order to bring these desires into physical manifestation by affirming:

> ➤ **I can and I will attract and draw to my life positive people, situations and circumstances that reflect and support my deepest goals and desires. In addition, I can and I will attract and draw to myself the love, joy, peace and great riches I truly desire and deserve. I Give Thanks!**

To think powerfully is to think, "I Am Powerful, Intelligent, Courageous and Beautiful" To think negative is to think, "I am a failure." Please remember, we attract and draw to ourselves our most dominant thoughts and beliefs. If it is our deepest intent to succeed in life, then we affirm the positive versus the negative, **"I Am The Greatest, I Look Great, I Feel Great, I Am Great."** In addition, we must dominate our every thought with Love, Joy, Peace and Great Riches. Not just for self, but for every person on this planet. Understanding and adopting this mindset/positive attitude will empower us to develop powerful thoughts, beliefs and behaviors that support and reflect our deepest goals and desires. Please note, this does not mean to ignore or deny the negative. However, if we focus on the positive versus the negative, eventually the positive will outweigh the negative. As a result, **we will attract and draw to ourselves a consistent flow of positive successes into our lives,** (Love, Joy, Peace and Great Riches).

Be optimistic, while at the same time, be aware of your strengths, weaknesses, opportunities and threats. This will allow you to effectively prepare your mind, body and spirit for Success Now.

What Do You Think? Notes, Comments, Commitments:

_____

_____

_____

What Do You Think? Notes, Comments, Commitments:

_____

_____

_____

_____

_____

_____

_____

_____

_____

What Do You Think? Notes, Comments, Commitments:

_____

_____

_____

Assignment

Here are some attitude changes that have healed and transformed lives in major ways. Check the ones that speak to you directly.

1. ____When I changed my attitude about people and started to have a positive conversation versus a negative conversation about them, my interactions with people became positive and uplifting. We really started to relate to one another on a higher level. Now, I am more confident and secure in my relationships with all people. In addition, it has allowed me to present and communicate more effectively in the world.

2. _____When I changed my attitude about being victimized as a young person, it empowered me to forgive them and myself. This allowed me to let go of a lot of guilt and shame. This concept has allowed me to heal and transform my life.

3. _____When I changed my attitude about my former relationship being over, and found peace with it, I attracted into my life a person who loves, respects and appreciates me. And, I truly love, respect, appreciate and enjoy them.

4. ____When I changed my attitude about my team member not stepping-up-to-the-plate, shortly thereafter we pulled together and landed a major two-year contract with a company we have been trying to secure for over 5 years.

5. ____When I changed my attitude about my spouse and children, they did not change. However, I do not allow

them to have power and control over me any longer. This has allowed me to focus on "doing what I need to heal and transform myself". My hope is that my light will begin to shine so brightly that my family will be attracted to it and be inspired to heal and transform their lives.

6. ____When I changed my attitude about losing everything and having to start over in life, it instantly made me feel better about moving forward. In addition, life started presenting powerful opportunities to me in a bold way. This gives me an inner "knowing" that everything is in divine order.

Questions & Answers

1. **What if I have a positive attitude but everyone around me has a negative attitude, and this influences me to have a negative attitude?** I say to you directly, "be clear on your intent and remember that you must make a decision to succeed in life, no matter what. Learn to let people do them, and you do you. If people want to hold on to negative attitudes, let them. But do not allow their negative attitudes to influence your positive attitude. And lastly, trust me, people with a negative attitude will eventually develop a positive attitude - if they intend to survive in the 21st Century." What do you think?

2. **I try to have a positive attitude about life, so why do things just keep going wrong for me?** Remember, a positive attitude is a universal law that promises to yield powerful results. In addition, a positive attitude is a requirement for success. Re-affirming this concept to yourself will motivate and empower you to keep moving

forward. Maintain a positive attitude and trust that this universal law will yield positive results beyond your wildest dreams. What do you think?

3. **I can have a positive attitude at work, so why is it that as soon as I get home with my family, it instantly turns negative?** Remember, it is easier to have a positive attitude in a controlled environment, but it is difficult to have a positive attitude in an out-of-control environment. What is the lesson? Learn how to have a positive attitude in an out-of-control environment. This will allow you to go to your next level of success. What do you think?

4. **Can you fake a positive attitude?** Yes, but you would only be fooling yourself. Truly successful people can always spot the fakers. Faking a positive attitude may get you an interview or the romantic date with him or her, but it will be short lived. Fakers are always eventually exposed. Instead of faking a positive attitude, refocus that energy on seeking a higher truth from within yourself. "Who do I desire to be and what do I desire to materialize in my life?" What do you think?

5. **How do you develop a positive attitude?** Re-Affirming your positive attitude affirmations will empower you to develop a stronger, more powerful attitude. This will give you a great start. What do you think?

I Surrender To My Higher Power

I Surrender To A Higher Power Within Myself

BE STILL AND KNOW THAT I AM POWERFUL

I am open and receptive to **discovering a higher power** within myself in order to achieve my highest Potential and Possibility.

I **forgive myself and other people** for any wrongdoings; therefore, I am free from guilt, shame and resentment.

I am open and receptive to **learning all that life has to teach** me, so that I am a stronger, more powerful person.

I am open and receptive to using my inner power to **heal and transform** my life to achieve my heart's desires.

I am open and receptive to overcoming my life challenges to **achieve the love, joy, peace and great riches** I truly desire and deserve.

I am open and receptive to overcoming my fears, doubts and insecurities, to **do what must be done** in order to **manifest my desires.**

I am open and receptive to **being a powerful person** to give great service and achieve my personal and professional goals and desires.

I Surrender To A Higher Power Within Myself!
BE STILL AND KNOW THAT I AM POWERFUL
I Give Thanks. I Give Thanks. I Give Thanks.

THE CENTER FOR MIND & ESTEEM DEVELOPMENT, INC.

RE-FOCUS: SUCCESS IS NOW

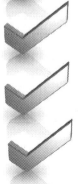

SELF-EMPOWERMENT

CHANGING FROM WITHIN

MY ENERGY

MY BARRIERS

SELF-LOVE

BELIEVING IN MYSELF

BY MARVIN MACK
YOUR PERSONAL DEVELOPMENT COACH

BONUS Membership Website: iampowerfulenough.com
Download Additional Self-Help eBooks, Audios & Videos FREE

It Is A Fact that success means nothing if our health is failing. If it is our intent to materialize successful romantic relationships, professional advancement or financial wealth, then our #1 goal must be to develop a healthier stronger mind, body and spirit. At this level of empowerment not only are we strong enough to overcome life challenges to succeed, but we are more open and receptive to attracting and drawing to ourselves our true goals and desires.

Fitting Exercise Into A Busy Schedule - You can find a way to add simple, quick exercises to your daily regimens for a slimmer waistline, increased energy, and a happier life.

Amazing Weight Loss & Health Tips and Discover 100 Ways to Lose 10 Pounds, Feel Better & Become Healthier ... - What you should always do before you sit down to eat if you really want to lose weight fast! What foods are good to eat -- and what foods you should stay away from at all costs!

Banish Bad Habits - How to free Yourself From Bad Habits, Forever - You'll learn how to replace your bad habits with healthy new habits. Focusing on your new lifestyle is like freeing the hand tied behind your back---suddenly you have power to bring about the change you desire.

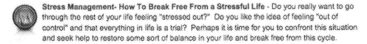

Stress Management- How To Break Free From a Stressful Life - Do you really want to go through the rest of your life feeling "stressed out?" Do you like the idea of feeling "out of control" and that everything in life is a trial? Perhaps it is time for you to confront this situation and seek help to restore some sort of balance in your life and break free from this cycle.

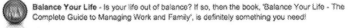

Balance Your Life - Is your life out of balance? If so, then the book, 'Balance Your Life - The Complete Guide to Managing Work and Family', is definitely something you need!

And Much More ...

Table of Contents

Copyright © by Marvin Mack
The Center For Mind & Esteem Development, Inc.
15 Charles Plaza
Baltimore, MD 21201
Iampowerfulenough.com
410-385-8978

Re-Focus: Success Is Now

4 Daily Renewals For Self-Empowerment

1. 4 Important Questions (A Self-Discovery Process)
2. I Am The Presence and the Power of Love
3. I Am The Greatest
4. I Am Empowered

A Template for "Discovering the Power Within Yourself"
4 Important Questions
You must ask and answer for yourself!

If you need some help getting started, please use the following template for discovering the power within yourself. (Again, you must come to your own revelations as to the meaning of these words in order for them to be effective in your life.)

Who am I? You are the presence and the power of love. Therefore, you are powerful beyond measure. Love is more powerful than anything or anyone that attempts to destroy it. This includes illness, negative people or situations, etc. As you come to this realization, you will be a more powerful person. This realization will allow you to overcome your life challenges, whatever they might be, and achieve authentic success.

What is My purpose in the world? Your main purpose is to discover how profoundly powerful you are to create Love, Joy, Peace and Great Riches in this world. Your purpose is to be Great and to share that greatness with the world. This attitude will show in the quality work that you do and the service you provide; be it at home, work or school. Whatever you do, you will do it with excellence.

What do I desire in order to be happy and successful? Your ultimate desire is to be a powerful person and to consistently experience love, joy, peace and prosperity. As these desires become your focus, you will begin to attract the external elements that you need – to be happy and successful. This is how you will achieve authentic success.

How should I overcome My life challenges in order to accomplish my goals? You are supposed to react and respond powerfully to negative situations and people. If your intention is to succeed, it will never matter the situation or person, you will deal with it powerfully.

I Am The Presence and the Power of Love

I Love Myself Unconditionally – My love for myself is not regulated by my successes, failures or who likes me or not. I love myself unconditionally because I am unconditional love. At this level of empowerment, I attract and draw to myself the love, joy, peace and great riches I truly desire and deserve.

I Am Responsible for My Life – I take full responsibility for healing and transforming my life to achieve my personal and professional goals and desires.

I Am Perfect Health – Every bone, muscle, tissue and cell of my body is filled with love and perfection. Therefore, I am eternally youthful, beautiful and in perfect health.

I Am Forgiving – I forgive myself and other people for any wrongdoings; therefore, I am free from guilt, shame and resentment. I have learned the lesson and now I am prepared to go to my next level of love, joy, peace and prosperity.

I Am Standing on Solid Ground – I am powerful enough to stop allowing negative people, situations and circumstances to have power and control over me. Therefore, there is nothing or no one that can stop me from loving, believing and having confidence in myself.

I Only Have Loving Relationships With Everyone (Family, Friends, Enemies, The World) - I love, respect and appreciate myself; therefore, I treat everyone with love and respect. I no longer feel the need to please people or understand why they do what they do. I accept people for who they are because I know who I Am. I give Love. I give Love. I give Love.

I Am Living my Life On Purpose – My main purpose is to discover how profoundly powerful I am to create Love, Joy, Peace and Great Riches in this world.

I Am Free, Free, Free – I am free because I know who I am, and I know that I can do all things with love that supports and strengthens me. Now, I operate at my fullest potential to achieve my personal and professional goals and desires.

In the name of Love, I am Love and I am willing to see and experience Love in this world.

I Am The Greatest

I Feel Great
I Look Great
I Am Great

I Am Powerful – I am spiritually, mentally and physically strong enough to overcome my life challenges to achieve my goals and desires. I am powerful enough to fulfill my purpose and achieve the love, joy, peace and great riches I truly desire and deserve!

I Am Intelligent - I have the brainpower to create, orchestrate and manifest greatness in my life. I learn and master any information or skill because I am a thinker and I use my brain to think. My mind is strong enough to visualize and manifest anything that my heart desires.

I Am Courageous – I fear nothing or no one. I am the presence and the power of love. Love is the most powerful force on earth. Therefore, I am powerful enough to overcome my fears, doubts and insecurities to achieve my heart's desires. I can do all things with love that supports and strengthens me.

I Am Unique – I am a special individual expression of love. Only I can do things the way that I do them. I add something extra special to this world.

I Am Beautiful – I am beautiful because I am the Presence and the Power of Love.

I Am The Greatest

I Feel Great! I Look Great! I Am Great!

I Give Thanks!

I Am Empowered

1. I plan, manage and organize myself to focus, execute, meet deadlines and achieve my daily goals and objectives.

2. I present and communicate myself confidently and effectively to get what I need from people.

3. I am mentally, emotionally and physically strong enough to overcome my life challenges, such as: multiple projects, energy crises and negative people.

4. I react and respond to all conflicts in a powerful manner.

5. I give quality service in a professional manner to be successful now.

6. I enjoy harmonious relationships with everyone: family, friends, enemies, and the world.

7. I love, respect and appreciate myself. I believe in myself. I believe that I will materialize my goals and desires.

8. I am open and receptive to discovering my highest potential to achieve the love, joy, peace and great riches I truly desire and deserve.

9. I am Energy. I am Passion. I am Free. I Am Empowered.

10. I give thanks. I give thanks. I give thanks.

Changing From The Inside Out

Master The Process of Change

- ❖ Changing From The Inside Out
  "Lose The Weight & Keep It Off"
- ❖ 5 Misperceptions About "Change"
- ❖ 5 Step Process for "Real Change"
- ❖ Conscious Living – A 5 Step Process

Lose The Weight & Keep It Off

"A short story about Getting to the root of the problem"

A few years ago I was overweight, unhealthy and angry. Even though I was successful professionally, I still felt like a failure because of the weight. I never saw myself gaining weight nor did I see myself starting to feel uncomfortable or unhappy with myself. I was 40 pounds overweight before I noticed the excess and my limitations because of the excess. Since I wanted to attract a romantic partner, and be socially accepted, I began a rigid diet and exercise routine. I curbed my intake of certain foods, and went to the gym 7 days a week. In 3 months, I lost 40 pounds.

My plan worked! People became attracted to me and I even attracted a romantic partner into my life. I was happy and I felt good. So good, I stopped going to the gym and started eating and drinking like everyone else. Within 9 months, I gained 20 pounds and my new clothes did not fit like they used to. Shortly thereafter, my romantic relationship was over, and friends stopped returning my calls. Within one year, I was right back to square one – overweight, lonely, frustrated and unhappy.

Six months later, I decided to jumpstart my life and try again. Monday morning was my start date and I was pumped and excited. I had my breakfast, which consisted of two pieces of toast and a cup of hot tea. For lunch I had a garden salad with low fat dressing.

By 1:30 p.m., my day was becoming stressful. Normally, I would push those stressful moments down by going to the vending machine for a candy bar and some vanilla cookies, but I was on a diet. By 3:30 p.m., I became more and more frustrated. I thought I was going to die. At 4:30 p.m., I found myself standing at the vending machine eating a candy bar and some cookies. When I became conscious that I abandoned my diet, I became completely disgusted with myself. "Forget it," I thought to myself. I didn't even make it to the gym. I was thoroughly disgusted with myself.

It was another six months and 10 pounds before I would try dieting again. This time I took a completely different approach. I started asking myself some hard questions like:

- ❖ *Why am I really overeating and destroying my body?*
- ❖ *Who am I changing for – myself or other people?*
- ❖ *What do I really want?*
- ❖ *What am I really afraid of?*
- ❖ *Why was I so angry?*
- ❖ *Do I really love, respect and appreciate myself?*

After spending some quality time answering these questions for myself, I began to analyze and address the root of my problems. I realized…

- ❖ I was overeating to relieve stress and to comfort myself.
- ❖ I was changing for other people, not myself.
- ❖ I really wanted love and acceptance.
- ❖ I feared change, rejection and disappointment.
- ❖ I realized that my anger was stemming from my un-forgiveness and resentment toward people from the past.
- ❖ I did not love, respect and appreciate myself as much as I thought.

As I began to address these issues one-by-one, I developed a stronger relationship with myself. I started preparing myself mentally, physically and spiritually to change my life. Within 8 months, I succeeded in losing the weight and keeping it off.

I Am Powerful Enough

I realized that I could not change myself for other people, because the harder I worked to befriend them, the harder I had to work to keep them. The more of myself I gave, the more they demanded. In this cycle, there was no more me, because I had lost myself. That was no way to live.

Eventually, I came to the realization that if I was going to change, I had to change for myself. This idea naturally gave me a consistent motivation to "be better." Slowly, I developed a stronger relationship with myself. It was this relationship that allowed me to feel comfortable and confident in myself. I naturally started handling negative people and situations in a more powerful way.

As I became more comfortable within myself, I naturally began to attract people who were comfortable with themselves and we became friends. So, ultimately when I changed from the inside out, I attracted into my life exactly what I wanted. The more I loved, respected and appreciated myself, the easier it became to change self-destructive habits.

The greatest lesson I learned about making the change – *Change starts within and I must be the number one reason I want to change.* As I began to love, respect and appreciate myself more, change came very easily and naturally.

5 Misperceptions About "Change"

1. ____ Change the outside and the inside will resolve itself. "I will feel better about myself when…." - Most people focus their attention on changing the outside: buy a new outfit, bigger house, landing a better job, more expensive material things, or get plastic surgery. "Now I feel better", they think. However, after the novelty wears off, they start to notice that same old incomplete feeling creeping back. Shortly thereafter, they are on the search for something else to jump-start their lives. If you desire to feel better about yourself, you must start from the inside and the outside will take care of it self.

2. ____ Change occurs overnight "I want success right now." – Change is a process that in most cases, takes time. So, prepare yourself to master patience. Don't beat yourself up if you do not succeed in your first, second or third attempt at changing. Relax and make a conscious decision that regardless of how many times you fail, you will never give up until you succeed at changing your life.

3. ____ Once you succeed at making the change, "you have arrived" – When you start to think that you have arrived, you have cut yourself off from growing. You are no longer open and receptive to the next level of success.   In some cases, you have not devised a solid plan to sustain the change, which may cause a relapse. Remember, there is always another level of success, love, joy, peace and prosperity you can aspire to achieve. You must relax in the process of life, because life is constantly changing and moving forward. Flow with it.

4. _____ You need other people to change in order for you to change – I remember being in a romantic relationship with this very nice woman. However, it seemed like all we did was argue and fight. One day I told her that I wanted our relationship to be more loving and peaceful. She agreed. It lasted two days before we were arguing again. I realized that I was unconsciously waiting for her to change first. Only after I made the conscious decision to stop arguing and fighting did the relationship became more loving and peaceful. When she finally realized that I was not going to participate, she stopped arguing.

Remember, if you want change in your relationships, you must change first and they will eventually follow. If they do not, at least *you* will have peace. Their absence will make room for people that are on your level.

5. _____ You need a healthy, supportive environment in order to change – Without question, your environment plays an important role in your ability to change your life. However, If you don't have the luxury of a healthy, supportive environment, does this give you a reason not to change in order to succeed? NO! Remember, your environment starts within your mind, body and spirit. When you start to develop your internal environment, via self-empowerment (a) you will find your external environment becoming healthier and more supportive, or (b) you will advance to a level where you are able to move to a healthier more supportive environment.

What Do You Think? Notes, Comments, Commitments:

_____
_____
_____

5 Step Process for "Real Change"

1. Relax, Relax, Relax – If you are not relaxed during the process of change, it makes the experience difficult and frustrating. When you are tense and frustrated, the needed positive energy cannot flow through you. When you are relaxed in the process of change, you naturally have a better attitude, are more energized, and feel empowered. This positive energy will make your process of change easier and more enjoyable, even in challenging times.

2. You must be the number one reason you want to change – Changing and altering yourself for others will only leave you feeling empty and unfulfilled in the end. You are worthy of being the number one reason you want to change your life. When you change because *you* want to change, it gives you an inner power and motivation that will last a lifetime.

3. You must start changing from the inside out – Whether you want to change your financial situation, relationships, career, or your physical body, you must start from the inside. As you begin to develop your mind, body and spirit you will become a more powerful person. This will give you the energy and confidence that you need to change your life externally. You will find yourself setting realistic goals, and following through on completing them one by one.

4. Start small, be consistent, and never give up – You must decide on what major changes you need to make in your life. Next, develop a written plan of action. Break your goals down into small tasks that you can work on each day. You must be consistent. Before you know it, you will have changed, reached your short-term goals and will be closer to your long-term or ultimate goals.

5. Live Consciously – There is no greater changing force than living consciously. Living consciously allows you to become aware of your mental, physical and emotional needs and make conscious decisions to deal with those needs in a healthy, empowering way. Living consciously will empower you to make effective decisions on a daily basis and react and respond to life's challenges in positive powerful ways.

SMALL SUCCESSES GIVE YOU MOTIVATION TO ACHIEVE THE LARGER SUCCESSES

What Do You Think? Notes, Comments, Commitments:

_____

_____

_____

_____

_____

_____

_____

Conscious Living - A 5 Step Process

Live consciously. The higher you are in consciousness, the less you allow negative forces to have power and control over you. You do not allow people or situations to steal your time and energy. When you live consciously, you have more time and energy to move forward and live your best life.

1. TURN DOWN THE NOISE

Turn off the television, the music and the people. You must spend quality time in silence so that you can hear your authentic inner voice speaking to you. Meditation is the greatest way to get in alignment with purpose and tap into a higher power within you. (It also helps you to do your daily chores in silence.)

2. ACKNOWLEDGE UNCONSCIOUS BEHAVIOR

Begin acknowledging when you are reacting and responding to life unconsciously. Being aware does not mean instant change. However, you will begin to see that you have a *choice*.

3. BE WILLING TO SEE LIFE DIFFERENTLY

Begin seeing life's negative people, situations and experiences in a positive way. Think powerfully. Ask yourself, "What is the opportunity, the blessing or lesson?" Learn to observe without judgment or getting emotionally caught-up in negative appearances. Sometimes, this can be a big challenge. However, it will force you to think differently. It is your *willingness* to think differently that will give you the power to overcome and rise above negative people and situations in order to succeed in life.

4. THINK BEFORE YOU REACT

Begin to think before you react and respond to any situation. This will save you a lot of time and energy. In most cases, overreacting

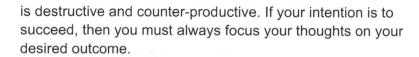

is destructive and counter-productive. If your intention is to succeed, then you must always focus your thoughts on your desired outcome.

5. REACT AND RESPOND IN A POSITIVE WAY

Begin handling all negative feelings, people or situations in a positive way and you will begin to see the total benefits of living consciously.

What Do You Think? Notes, Comments, Commitments:

_____

_____

_____

_____

_____

_____

_____

What Do You Think? Notes, Comments, Commitments:

_____

_____

_____

_____

_____

_____

_____

_____

Success Misperceptions

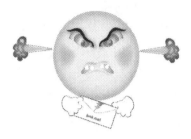

We are conditioned by the world around us to seek personal fulfillment and success outside of ourselves. Money, power, relationships, career, and material possessions are props that we have been told will bring us lasting satisfaction and success. And they do… for about as long as a good meal lasts. The joyful sensations that come from, "I finally got that (_?_) I always wanted" are as fleeting as the glimpse of a fairy in a dark forest. Before you comprehend what is happening – you will be hungry for something else, for something more, to fill the void.

Before long, you will return to a state of "I need something more to make me happy and successful." You will again seek those outward things, which you believe will bring you lasting success and happiness. As a result, you may develop some misperceptions and self-defeating habits about success and achieving it. Meanwhile, you may feel frustrated and overwhelmed with no sense of direction. You may blame your failures on situations and people. You may even believe that your inability to achieve success comes from some innate character trait that cannot be changed. I argue that your inability to achieve success may be due to your misperceptions about success.

As you read the 10 misperceptions about success, place a check mark beside the misperceptions you may be holding on to.

_____ 1. **"Success will fulfill me and make me happy."** Have you ever said, "Once I achieve this goal, I will be happy and successful - Then I can relax." Have you ever achieved something you have always wanted? This could be graduating, landing a great job, finding the love of your life, having a child, buying a house or car, etc. More than likely, your answer is, "yes." You were smiling for days, but did the feeling last? Yes or No - Why? External success will only fulfill and make you happy for a short period of time. Lasting fulfillment and happiness comes from thinking powerfully, loving yourself and believing in your ability to set and accomplish any goal you desire.

_____ 2. **The reason *I am not* successful is because of extenuating circumstances** (negative people, situations and circumstances) – Have you ever failed at completing a task and then blamed the failure on someone or something else? This is one of the biggest misperceptions about achieving success. The more you realize that you are powerful beyond measure, you will find yourself succeeding more and more regardless of extenuating circumstances. Always remember, at every level of success there will be negative situations and people that you will have to confront. The key is to learn how to effectively deal with your life challenges, NOW. This will make you a stronger person to overcome extenuating circumstances, now and in the future, to achieve your goals.

_____ 3. **You must be a selfish, ruthless person in order to achieve success in today's world.** Have you ever said "no" to someone, only to have the person label you as a mean, ruthless person? Yes or No - Did you start to feel guilty and think you were a bad person? Remember, you must not confuse making right decisions with being selfish or ruthless. When you decide to say "no" to someone, you may be viewed as a ruthless, selfish person but don't take it Personally. If your intention is to succeed and your intuition is telling you to say "no", then say "No". You have the power within you to make the right decisions based on what is best for you and the benefit of the whole.

_____ 4. **"When I achieve success, then people will respect and appreciate me." Is this your belief?** Yes or No - Without question, when things are good, a flock of people will love, respect and appreciate you. However, there is another flock of people who will envy and even hate you because of your success. Remember, there are two sides to achieving success – a negative side, and a positive side. When we achieve success, and we do not anticipate the negative sides of the equation, that success is soon undermined by negativity. Thus, even when you get the success you want, you won't feel happy or successful. If you desire for people to respect and appreciate you, then love yourself unconditionally and people will naturally love, respect and appreciate you.

_____ 5. **Successful people do not make mistakes.** Do you feel like a failure because of some past mistakes you may have made? Yes or No - Please remember, successful people and people who love and believe in themselves make mistakes. However, they do not keep repeating the same mistakes over and over, expecting a different result each time. Truly successful people learn from their mistakes and keep moving forward. If your intention is to succeed, then learn from your mistakes and use them as an opportunity to grow.

_____ 6. **"When I am Successful, I will not have any problems or challenges."** Are you effectively dealing with your life challenges now? Yes or No - This is one of the most prevalent misperceptions about success. Hear this loud and clear - every level of success has its challenges. In light of this, you must learn how to effectively deal with your life's negative challenges in a powerful manner, now. When you do not believe you have the power to overcome a life challenge, remember, there is a higher power within you that can. Turn to it.

____ 7. **External success builds my self-esteem / self-worth and value. Do you have high self-esteem?** Yes or No - Your level of self-esteem is based on how you feel about yourself at any given time. It is a mistake to let your current level of achievements determine your present self-esteem, self-worth and value. The healthiest way to build high self-esteem is by 1) learning to love and believe in yourself more and 2) staying focused on creating the life you ultimately desire to live.

____ 8. **"If I look successful, then I am successful." Is this your belief?** There are many people who have accomplished all the external successes of their dreams. They are viewed by society as being very successful. However, in some cases, after looking beyond the external success, what you see is a fearful person in the process of self-destructing; they live with severe anxiety or depression. Do not fall into this trap. Remember, you must not only look successful, but also be and live successfully.

_____ 9. **"I must 'know the right people' to be successful." Is this your belief?** Yes or No - Remember, it is great when you know the right people. However, if you do not know the right people, do not allow it to stop you from moving forward on your goals. With today's technology (via computers, the internet and networking organizations) it is much easier to advertise and promote your product or service around the world. If you truly believe in yourself, with persistence, you will be successful.

_____ 10. Other:

_____

_____

_____

If you are guilty of holding any of these negative beliefs, GIVE THEM UP! (Flush them down the toilet.) Negative beliefs steal your energy and keep you from operating at your fullest potential to achieve your personal and professional goals.

Whenever you start to feel frustrated or overwhelmed because you have not achieved the level of success you desire, I encourage you to review these 10 misperceptions about success. This will help you to put success in the right perspective.

What Do You Think? Notes, Comments, Commitments:

_____

_____

_____

_____

_____

_____

_____

_____

Identify Your "ROOT BARRIERS" To Success

You have tried everything to succeed, but continue to fail. You have everything that you need to succeed, but continue to fail. You feel empowered when you achieve occasional success, but shortly thereafter, your success and happiness are sabotaged. If this is you, begin to identify your Root Barriers to success. Root barriers are blind spots that keep you from achieving success, now. When you can identify your root barriers to success, you are able to confront and resolve what is really standing in your way of success.

Once the mind determines there is no value in holding on to these internal barriers, it will begin the process of dismantling the internal thought processes that no longer have value or worth. At this point, you will then free yourself to think clearly, re-energize, make effective decision and produce powerful results in your daily life.

Identify your root barriers and begin the process of healing and transforming your life beyond your wildest dreams.

____ 1. **5 Major Fears** (Negative emotions caused by an expectation of danger)

Fear of Success	People will expect more of you and your life will become more demanding and challenging.
Fear of Failure or Poverty	The pain of past failures is blocking you from trying again, and again.
Fear of Change	Change requires starting over and you just don't have the energy.
Fear of the Unknown	You don't know what to expect, so you stay in your comfort zone.
Fear of Rejection	The pain of hearing "no" hurts too bad, so you stop trying.
Fear of Humiliation	People will laugh at you, criticize and ridicule you.

You can overcome your fears, doubts and insecurities by re-affirming your power, surrendering to a higher power greater than yourself and by consistently doing something positive on a daily basis to move your life forward.

____ 2. **5 Negative Thoughts Leading to Negative Beliefs:**
"I don't believe or have confidence in myself."
"People are always holding me back from success."
"I need someone to help me."
"I need more money, education, a better physical appearance."
"I am not worthy of love, joy, peace or success."

These negative beliefs can be completed eliminated by re-affirming your power as often as possible. This will allow you to transform your negative beliefs into positive beliefs that will support you in your growth and development process.

___ 3. **Denial** – an inability to see the truth. When you lie to yourself about the root of your problems, you are blocking yourself from moving forward. You may even say, "I love myself and I don't need to change." Yet you continue to unconsciously destroy yourself. Some major problems that you may deny include: low performance, the abuse of food, alcohol or drugs, abusive relationships, unhealed pain or un-forgiveness. You must begin to acknowledge your barriers in order to resolve them and reach your next level of success.

___ 4. **Limited Comfort Zone** – Have you become comfortable with *mediocrity*? When you are comfortable with a negative, limited way of living, there is no motivation to move forward. People who become comfortable with mediocrity and limitation can never become truly successful. You must always remember two things: (1) there is a power within you that you must begin to exercise and (2) the world is filled with endless possibilities and opportunities if you are willing to step outside of your comfort zone to encounter them.

___ 5. **Abused** – People who were abused often develop negative beliefs about themselves. If this is you, you may think, "I can't...I am not worthy of success," "Maybe I deserved the abuse because I am a bad person," or, "I am a victim, and I cannot protect myself." Once you start entertaining these negative thoughts and ideas, you unconsciously stop believing in your ability to succeed. In order to achieve authentic success, these inner conflicts must be resolved and healed.

___ 6. **Negative opinions of Family, Society and Peers** – Constantly worrying about what people think of you can drain valuable energy and can instill self-doubt. People may say to you, "You cannot accomplish that goal. Your feelings or ideas are not valid." If you do not know that you are powerful beyond measure, you could conform to their negative opinions and choose not to accomplish the goal. You can listen to others' opinions; however,

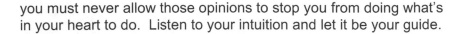

you must never allow those opinions to stop you from doing what's in your heart to do. Listen to your intuition and let it be your guide.

____ 7. **Indecisiveness** – anything not clearly defined, which amounts to inconsistent behaviors. If today you want this, then tomorrow you want that, and the following day something else, you are indecisive. If you cannot focus on what you desire out of life, you are indecisive. If you cannot give a direct answer about what accomplishments would make you happy, you are indecisive. The more you crystallize your direction in life, the easier it is to make decisions and be consistent.

____ 8. **The Blame Game** – "They (parents, family, friends, supervisor, etc) are the reason I am not successful." People who refuse to take responsibility for their lives can never become truly successful. If this describes you, acknowledge that there will always be negative situations and persons who will attempt to discourage you. If you are going to be successful, you must take full responsibility for your life. Even though we are not responsible for the challenges that come to us, we are responsible for our reaction and response to them. When you stop blaming others and start taking personal responsibility, you embrace the power within you to transcend negative situations and people.

____ 9. **No Discipline** – If you can't seem to focus or be patient enough to complete a small task, it may be due to a lack of discipline. If you lack discipline, you will find it difficult to achieve success. The reason is that you must first be able to focus to complete the small tasks that compound and lead to your ultimate goals. You have the power within you to be disciplined. Tap into it.

____ 10. **Negative Drama** – Do you find yourself constantly talking negatively about other people? Or, do you find yourself always being mixed up in some "he said, she said" gossip? If so, you may be using negative drama to avoid focusing on achieving your personal and professional goals. You must come to a realization that negative drama is not going to help you achieve success.

Therefore, you must learn to avoid participating in any negative drama and focus on achieving your goals.

____ 11. **Mr. or Ms. "Know It All"** – These are the people who are not open and receptive to what they don't know because they think they know it all. And they usually don't. If you fall into this category, and think you know it all, realize that you have unconsciously cut yourself off from growth. If you are going to achieve your next level of success, you must be open and receptive to what you do not know. You must always seek a greater realization of power, love, joy, peace and wealth.

____ 12. **Lack of Focus and Vision** – People who do not know where they are going in life usually go nowhere. You must have a clear mental picture of exactly what you desire to accomplish in your life. Next, you must use all your time and energy accomplishing those goals. In addition, eliminate all negative things, situations and people that do not fall in alignment with the accomplishment of your goals.

____ 13. **No Energy** – People who procrastinate and are not productive are usually sapped of physical energy. Their lives are usually filled with energy drainers. Energy drainers are negative people or situations that steal your energy. You must learn to (1) protect and conserve your energy supply and (2) focus your energy on accomplishing your personal goals.

____ 14. **Baggage** – Baggage consists of negative feelings and attitudes, such as: hidden addictions, anger, not being open and receptive, un-forgiveness, unworthiness issues, or the need to "always be right or feel superior." People who are carrying a lot of negative baggage cannot move forward. If you are going to be successful, you must unload your baggage. You can achieve this by living yourself more consciously. Who do you desire to be and what do you desire to create? Now focus on that.

____ 15. **Consumed with everyone else's needs and wants.**
Do you feel overwhelmed because you are consumed by everyone else's needs and wants?   Do you feel you have no time or energy left to take care of your own needs; moreover, you just can't say, "no" to people?   People who are consumed with others' needs and wants eventually begin to lose themselves. As a result, they usually do not achieve their personal or professional goals. If your intention is to be successful, then you must 1) put yourself first, 2) learn to say "no," to people, and 3) allow others to learn how to take care of themselves.

____ 16. **"Yes, But"** – You have been given a powerful success concept that promises to revolutionize your life. Moreover, you have been given specific instructions on how to implement the concept. The idea has worked for everyone and is guaranteed to work for you. You know that implementing the idea will revolutionize your life. As soon as you say, "Yes, but," you have given yourself an excuse not to implement the concept. If you are going to be successful, you must move your big "BUT" out of the way and "just do it."

____ 17. **"I just don't know what I should do"** - Are you constantly saying this to yourself? Could it be true that you do know, but you just do not have the courage to follow through on that knowing? Yes or No? In most cases we know exactly what we need to do, but we don't do it. The reasons usually stem from our fears, doubts and insecurities. Meaning, we just do not have the courage to do it. This internal conflict can go on for long periods of time.

____ 18. **"Inability to let go of bad influences"** - Do you have bad influences, such as negative people or bad habits, in your life that you just can't seem to let go of? If so, please realize that before you can have the energy and focus required for success, you must take back your power from these bad influences. You know they are bad influences because they consistently drain your energy and take you off focus. The next time you observe yourself being overcome by a bad influence, I encourage you to get in the habit of saying, "No, Not Today". Next refocus yourself on being who you desire to be and creating what you desire to create in your life. Each time you do this, you will become stronger and stronger within yourself to succeed.

____ 19. **Addictions** - Are you addicted to food, drugs, alcohol, sex, abuse, or negative drama?   If so, please realize that before you can think clearly, make effective decisions and have the energy to produce powerful results in your life – the addiction must be eliminated. There are many techniques and programs to overcome an addiction. I recommend 1) learning to love, respect and appreciate yourself more, 2) surrendering to a higher power greater than yourself, 3) developing your belief and confidence within yourself and 4) refocusing your time, energy and thoughts on creating the life you ultimately desire to live. Remember, think about your possibility and potential. Other people have completely overcome their addictions and so can you.

____20. **The Saboteur & Feeling Un-Worthy** - A person who caries out an act of sabotage – Have you ever received something that you truly desired, then, consciously or un-consciously, you sabotaged it to the point it was taken away from you? Do you believe that you are worthy of the love, joy, peace and great riches? When you observe yourself sabotaging yourself in any way, I encourage you to affirm to yourself, " I am worthy of the love, joy, peace and great riches I truly desire and deserve, period." This will help you to realize that regardless of the past, present or future, you have the power to attract and draw to yourself the life you truly desire and deserve.

These internal barriers are what trigger FAILURE MECHANISMS and you start to feel:

Frustrated – You become disappointed with life because you don't have what you desire.

Angry – You are angry because someone has hurt or disappointed you. Anger is a negative emotion that steals your energy, joy and peace of mind.

Ignorant – Your ignorance stems from a failure to know how powerful you really are. When you are ignorant to your own power, you respond to negative challenges in fear.

Limited – Your perceived limitations are created based on the appearance of lack. When you are limited in your thinking, you are not open to possibilities.

Uncertain – Your uncertainty stems from your inability to meditate long enough to listen to your intuition. When you are uncertain, you procrastinate.

Resentful – Your resentment stems from what you feel people have done to you. When you have resentment, your annoyance and distrust of people shows in your presentation and communication skills.

Escapism – You may escape into food, drugs, alcohol, sex, television, video games, other people's affairs, etc. You escape from yourself in order to avoid your pain and negative feelings. You also escape realizing your highest potential.

Each time you observe yourself procrastinating, making excuses or feeling powerless, I encourage you to identify your root barriers and affirm to yourself, "I am powerful enough to overcome and eliminate my barrier and failure mechanism." This will empower you to discover with power within to overcome and eliminate your internal barriers and failure mechanisms to materialize positive results in your daily life. Applying and practicing these techniques will help you to think more clearly and will dramatically increase your energy level and improve the overall quality of your life.

What Do You Think? Notes, Comments, Commitments:

_____

_____

_____

_____

_____

_____

_____

_____

What Do You Think? Notes, Comments, Commitments:

_____

_____

_____

_____

_____

_____

_____

_____

Energy!

Energy is the capacity for action and for doing work.
- Law of Physics

If you have energy:
- o   You think clearly and make effective decisions
- o   You overcome life challenges powerfully
- o   You present and communicate yourself effectively
- o   You get along harmoniously with all people
- o   You attract and draw to yourself opportunities
- o   You are constantly moving your life forward

If you don't have energy:
- o   You procrastinate for long periods of time
- o   You constantly make excuses
- o   You do not attempt to try new things
- o   You can't present and communicate yourself effectively
- o   You may spend most of your time lying around doing nothing for the rest of your life

I Am Powerful Enough

Success & Energy

Your energy level affects every area of your life. If you are going to be successful in life, you must be energized.

Employment & Energy

If you want to be hired, be successful on the job, or get promoted, you must be energized. Employers want employees who are optimistic, professional, knowledgeable and willing to go the extra mile. People who are self-motivated, efficient and excited about their job are the people who get hired and promoted within the company.

Financial Success and Energy

If you want to achieve financial stability/freedom, you must be energized. The amount of money you are receiving today is a reflection of the amount of energy you are giving. Money is an exchange for energy. The more energy you give, the more money you will make.

Successful Relationships & Energy

If you want to attract positive people into your life, you must be energized. When you see someone for the first time, the first thing you notice is his or her energy level. Light attracts light. The same is true in relationship. If you are an uplifting, energetic person, with a positive attitude, you will attract people with similar personalities. Moreover, people will like and respect you.

Healthy Environment & Energy

If you want a clean and organized environment, you must be energized. Your environment is a direct reflection of your mental and emotional state. It has been scientifically proven that when your environment is clean and organized, you can think more clearly and manage your emotions more effectively.

Positive Self-Image & Energy

If you want to look good and feel good about yourself, you must be energized. Your energy level is reflected in your self-image and presentation to the world. When you feel good, you look good and do good. A positive self-image consists of presenting yourself as a person with power, intelligence, courage and beauty. Moreover, it does not matter what your position is in life. Regardless of where you are in your life today, you must present yourself as a powerful person in order to achieve success.

What Do You Think? Notes, Comments, Commitments:

_____

_____

_____

_____

_____

_____

_____

6 Symptoms of an Energy Crisis

Are you in an energy crisis?

Most of us experience at least one of these six warning signs of an energy crisis long before we are painfully energy deficient. Yet we typically ignore these symptoms. We are often so consumed with the burdens of daily living that we ignore our own feelings, emotions and physical needs. In most cases we wait until we are overwhelmed, exhausted and totally wiped out before we realize that we are in an energy crisis. Check off the following symptoms that apply to you:

___1. "I don't feel like it"

Is this your attitude everyday? If so, you are energy deficient. In most cases your energy level is low and now your body is telling you, "I need you to take better care of me." If you do not listen to your body, eventually it will shut down completely and you will have no energy.

___2. Living life in the dark

Do you feel dull and out of focus? Are you always running late, missing appointments, forgetting to do things, and playing catch-up? Do you have difficulty concentrating, focusing and thinking logically? When you are unable to solve simple problems in your daily life, this is a definite indication that you are running out of brainpower/energy.

___3. **Substance Abuse (food, alcohol, drugs, etc.)**

Do you constantly feel tired, sluggish and fatigued? As your body starts its descent into low energy around 10:00 a.m., do you start thinking, "I need something to pick me up?" This pattern of thinking usually turns into an addiction or bad habit. It may boost your energy level for that moment, but the long-term effects are destructive to your body. You start needing more and more doses to satisfy your craving and to boost your energy level. This is how five cigarettes a day turn into two packs a day, or two beers a night, turns into drinking a six-pack of beer before 9:00 a.m. One sleeping pill a few nights a week turns into every night needing two sleeping pills and a few shots of cognac, just to go to sleep. This does not include the pills you need to get up every morning.

___4. **Chronic Unhappiness**

Are you walking around like a zombie? Do you have this "victim" look on your face everyday? Are people always asking you, "What's wrong? It can't be that bad." When something great happens is everyone happy and excited, except you? Do you instead sit there unable or unwilling to enjoy the moment?

___5. **Unmotivated**

Do you have no desire to do anything other than what you must do to "get through the day?" Is your life centered on doing as little as possible, including improving yourself? Are you only motivated to escape into The Young and the Restless or Jerry Springer?

___6. **Antisocial**

Do you shy away from being around or communicating with other people? Do you avoid eye contact with anyone because they will see the inner hurt, pain and disgust you feel about yourself? Do you fear criticism and judgment from people?

Identify Your Energy Drainers

Energy thieves are negative things or people that steal your energy; they leave you feeling drained and powerless. Even though energy thieves may seem harmless, over time they negatively alter and control your life. The more energy thieves take from you, the less energy you have to create the life you desire to live. You are then unable to be motivated or productive. Moreover, you cannot enjoy life. Below are some typically energy thieves. Identify your energy drainers and begin the process of eliminating them. Ultimately you will find yourself having more energy to be who you desire to be and create the life you desire.

___1. Negative People
Have you noticed that when you are in the company of certain people, you are left feeling tired and drained? These people are called energy drainers or joy killers. They thrive on complaining and stealing other people's energy with their negative drama and need for constant attention. Unfortunately, these people can be your mother-in-law or your supervisor. Moreover, if you are a "people pleaser," or "co-dependent" on energy drainers, you feel

you have no choice but to allow them to drain your energy because you believe you need them in order to survive.

___2. Unconscious Living

You make the same mistakes over and over because you are not aware of how you feel and what you are doing. You do not acknowledge the things that are not working in your life and are stealing your energy. Your mantra is, "I just don't understand why my life is not working and why I am not at my next level of successful."

___3. Other People's Successes

You are envious and jealous of other people's success. You secretly resent successful people, like Oprah, the Obamas, or Donald Trump, because they started out with the same obstacles in life as you did, but they became successful while you did not. Your friend and coworker gets a promotion and you don't. You are smiling on the outside, but inside you are furious. Next, you are making negative comments about your ex-friend and coworker behind their back.

___4. Worrying

Your life is one big anxiety attack. You worry from the time you wake up every morning, until you fall asleep at night. You worry about everything – the future, the past, your health, money, relationships, love, romance, negative experiences, what people think about you, etc. Your mantra is, "What am I going to do? What is going to happen?" Constantly, you ask anyone who will listen, "What should I do?" You spend more time worrying and talking about your problems than you spend doing anything to resolve them. You could run a major corporation on the time and energy you spend worrying.

___5. Keeping up with the Joneses

The Joneses are the people who live up the street from you. Only they have more money, a bigger home, sleeker car, the finest clothes and every material item you desire. They are always first to buy the latest fad on the market to make their lives more appealing. In an attempt to keep up with the Joneses, you must be the second in line to buy the latest fad, even if you cannot afford it. So what if you must charge it, mortgage your home, spend your life's savings or take from the children's college tuition? As long as you look good on the outside, it does not matter if you are poor, internally stressed, frustrated, unfulfilled and dead. You convince yourself, "At least I look good on the outside, people will think I am rich. That is all that matters, right?"

___6. Indecisiveness
You can't make a decision about something and stick to it. So you avoid having to decide by not doing anything. Even though the issue is in the forefront of your mind, you cannot commit to making a decision. Ten years go by and you still have not decided to leave that abusive relationship or dead end job you constantly complain about.

___7. Negative Addictions
This could be an addiction to food, drugs, alcohol, sex, etc. When you have an addiction to something or someone, it consumes and steals most, if not all, of your energy. You feel you have no control over your life because all you can think about is getting your next "fix." The hidden hazard about any addiction is the belief that you do not have a problem. An addiction is a problem that eventually destroys you. Unfortunately, people never see the DANGER until it is too late.

___8. Avoidance Mechanisms
From cooking and cleaning, to going to work, we all have responsibilities throughout the day that we must do. However, some people spend more time thinking about how much they hate doing it than the time it takes to do it.

___9. Needing a Relationship
When am I going to get married, find someone who will love, respect and appreciate me, someone who will take care of me?

Aside from daily responsibilities, romantic relationships are a high priority for most people. They spend countless hours, days, and nights searching for that someone special. For some people, that is all they can think about. They enter into relationship after relationship only to find themselves losing energy, and part of themselves.

___10. Gossiping

Whether you are gossiping about someone else or they are gossiping about you, it is energy draining. Worrying about what other people think of you will not bring you closer to your goal. Likewise, worrying about other people's personal business will not help you reach your goals.

What Do You Think? Notes, Comments, Commitments:

_____

_____

_____

_____

_____

_____

_____

_____

What Do You Think? Notes, Comments, Commitments:

_____

_____

_____

_____

How To Re-Energize

WHERE DOES YOUR TIME, ENERGY & THOUGHTS GO?

Family and Friends	_____%
Job or Worrying about a job	_____%
Leisure time (watching television, going to nightclubs, etc.)	_____%
Educational (reading, writing, learning, etc)	_____%
Self-Empowerment (Personal & Professional Development)	_____%

Three of the biggest mistakes people make regarding where they focus their time, energy and thoughts:

1. They do not consciously know where most of their time, energy and thoughts are going. These are the people who are still asking themselves the question, "Why am I so tired?" or "Why have I not reached the next level of success?"

2. They focus their energy on non-productive things and people. These people are still in denial about what is really important in their lives. Moreover, they allow negative things and people to steal their time and energy. People use this technique to take the focus off themselves so they do not have to think about their desires or future. Their anthem is, "I have no time or energy." This gives them an excuse to avoid going to the next level of success.

3. They believe they have no control over where they spend their time, energy and thoughts. These are the people who usually have a victim mentality and do not believe in themselves.

When your energy level is low, it dramatically affects your life. It diminishes your ability to be productive, communicate well with people, handle crisis, create more Health, Relationships, Professional Advancement and Financial Wealth. When you are energy deficient, you are unable to receive true love, joy, peace and prosperity into your life. What do you think?

How To Re-direct Your Time, Energy & Thoughts:

1. Consciously evaluate and know where most of your time, energy and thoughts are going. When you consciously know where your time, energy and thoughts are going, you are focused on who you desire to be and what you desire to create. Moreover, you make better decisions. In every situation that is taking you off focus, you must ask yourself, "Is this really worth my time, energy, and thought?"

2. Focus and place your time, energy and thoughts on productive things and people. When you know what you want and where you are going in life, most of your energy is focused on accomplishing those goals. You naturally do not allow non-productive things and people to steal your time and energy or take you off focus.

3. Understand that you are in control of where you focus and place your time, energy and thoughts. It starts with believing and having confidence in your ability to say "Yes" or "No" and mean it. Always focus your time, energy and thoughts on positive, productive activities that will bring you closer to your desired goals in life.

Energy Boosters for Your Mind, Body & Spirit

3 Major ENERGY SOURCES

1. Mind

"The Ultimate CEO/President." The mind acts as the energy force that is in charge of telling your belief system, emotions and body what to do. The mind manages and organizes the details of what needs to be done and how it needs to be done. Then it tells the body exactly what to do. Everything that you see around you, aside from what nature created, was first created in the mind system of a person. You must use your mind to create greatness in your life.

2. Body

"The Ultimate Machine." The body acts as the energy force that does the physical work needed to accomplish your goals. The body is one of your most important tools; at best, it can do and create anything you desire. Conversely, if you don't sustain a healthy

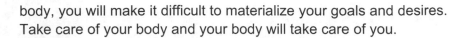

body, you will make it difficult to materialize your goals and desires. Take care of your body and your body will take care of you.

3. Spirit

"The Ultimate Motivator." The Spirit is an invisible force of energy that motivates and inspires you to create and give life to an idea on a physical level. Tapping into this energy source allows you to connect with a higher source of power within you that is more powerful than anything or anyone in this world. You must tap into the power of your spirit to overcome major obstacles in the path to achieve greatness in your life

Ultimately, the mind, body and spirit are supposed to work together to fulfill your divine purpose on this earth. If any one of these elements is lacking in doing their job, the goal is usually not met. Do not wait until you hit "rock bottom" before you decide to develop your mind, body and spirit. To get the best results from each, everyday you must spend quality time exercising and developing your three sources of energy, Your Mind, Body & Spirit.

What Do You Think? Notes, Comments, Commitments:

_____

_____

_____

_____

_____

_____

_____

_____

TECHNIQUE #1:

Meditation for Spiritual Development

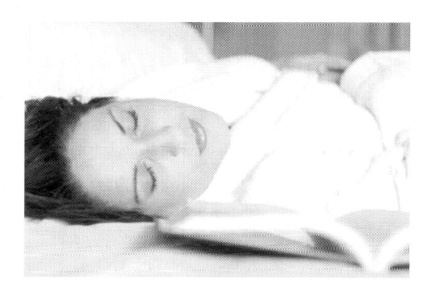

Meditation means sitting in silence and contemplating the truth about who you are, your purpose and your desires. Meditation allows you to tap into the highest source of energy inside yourself. It relaxes you, reduces stress, and increases your ability to focus, listen, and become a stronger more powerful person. Meditating regularly will help to center and balance your mind, body, and spirit. Consistent meditation will move you to a better overall state of health.

Also, Meditation will dramatically increase your spiritual development. Prayer is love and love is one of the most powerful forces in the world. Meditation and prayer are absolutely necessary to overcome life challenges in order to succeed.

Meditation Exercise:

Get in a comfortable position sitting or lying down, make sure your back is relatively straight. Your eyes may be opened or closed.

Breathe in and out through your nose and allow your breathing to slow down slightly, letting it be natural and comfortable. As you breathe in, feel your lungs fill from the bottom to the top. Breathing out, empty your lungs from top to bottom. Focus your attention on a spot in the center of your belly about an inch below your navel and in the center of your body; this is a very important part of the exercise. It helps you feel grounded and connected to your inner power. As you inhale, feel your diaphragm – sheet of muscle between your lungs and your abdomen – being pulled down toward the center of your belly. As you exhale, feel your diaphragm return to its natural position.

If you have trouble meditating, try taking an affirmation into your meditation, such as "I am Love," "I Am Joy," "I am Peace," or "I Am Rich." Repeating these affirmations will allow your mind, body and spirit to focus on the realization and manifestation of these powerful words. Moreover, you will produce positive results in your life. At this level of empowerment, you will heal and transform your life and begin to attract and draw to yourself the life you ultimately desire and deserve.

You can do this affirmation meditation anywhere: at home, in your car, on a bus, or standing in line, etc. Do this exercise daily for 5 to 15 minutes per sitting, and it will energize and renew your mind, body and spirit.

TECHNIQUE #2:
Affirm: No More Drama
Re-Focus On Your Highest Potential & Possibility
<u>Check Yourself</u>

1. ___No more Blaming and not taking responsibility for your Success and no more playing the victim! (It no longer works.)

2. ___No more complaining, sitting in judgment, or gossiping! (Stop Negative inner and outer conversations, Re-focus that energy on creating your highest potential & possibility.)

3. ___No more living in denial and not confronting reality! It only prolongs your growth. (The truth will set you free.)

4. ___ No more being unprofessional and thinking it is funny! (It is no longer worth it; you want people's respect.)

5. ___No more getting caught up in other people's dramas! No more power struggles or playing mental games with people. (Re-focus that energy on fulfilling your purpose.)

6. ___ No more being greedy, needy and un-grateful. (Being grateful will draw to you your greatest good.)

7. ___ No more sabotaging your successes. (You are worthy of the love, joy, peace and prosperity that you truly desire.)

8. ___ No more thinking that you are entitled to something without working for it. (You must get in the habit of working hard for what you truly desire.)

9. ___ No more thinking that you can be mean and underhanded with other people and still succeed in life. (Treat all people with love and respect and you will succeed many times over.)

10. ___No more thinking that you are not good enough! (We are all worthy of Love, Joy, Peace and Prosperity. This Include you.)

TECHNIQUE #3:
"I Am Energy" The Power of Words

Positive affirmations are positive words, thoughts or ideas you recite in order to produce a desired result, goal or intention. When your energy is low, a negative conversation starts to develop – "I am tired. I can't go on. I can't do it." You must replace these negative thoughts with positive thoughts. Remember that your thoughts motivate what you believe, how you feel and what you do and produce. Even if you do feel tired, you must affirm to yourself that you have the energy to fulfill your purpose and achieve your goals and desire. The following affirmations will give you a boost of energy when you start to feel powerless or drained of your energy.

4 Powerful Affirmations to Boost Your Energy Level:

1. I have an unlimited amount of energy.

When you start to feel overwhelmed by daily tasks, saying this affirmation will relax your mind, freeing you of stress and worry. This relief will allow you to re-focus, regain your power and do what needs to be done in order to move your life forward.

2. I am a powerful force of energy.

When you are faced with negative forces or obstacles coming against you, saying this affirmation will empower your mind to focus on solutions to overcome the challenge. When your mind is empowered, it feels equipped and strong enough to conquer the world to achieve its goals.

3. I can. I will. It is done.

When you start feeling frustrated because you failed or are heading in that direction, saying this affirmation will restore your belief and self-confidence. Affirming and knowing your capability will motivate and give you the energy to push forward until you succeed.

4. I can do anything.

When you start to feel as though you cannot do something, or a project seems overwhelming, saying this affirmation will empower your mind to get the job done. When you think positive thoughts and have a good attitude, you are tapping into a powerful source of energy that will help you to achieve your goals.

I Am Powerful Enough

TECHNIQUE #4:

Tips For Handling Your "Energy Drainers"

ENERGY DRAINERS	TIPS TO SURMOUNT OBSTACLES
Overcome by negative people	If you cannot avoid them, become emotionless in their presence. Let them do or say whatever they want, but don't respond. When they see they can no longer affect you, they will try harder, but eventually they will stop. Moreover, you must stop setting yourself up to depend on negative people. Be responsible for taking care of yourself and accomplishing your own goals and desires.
Living Unconsciously	Notice that the first sign of living unconsciously is when you start to feel off-balanced, out of focus, incomplete or negative. These are red flags for you to become conscious to the fact that you are responsible for how you feel and how you react and respond to life. You have the power enough to rise above all negativity.
Consumed by other people's success	You must be inspired, instead of resentful, by other people's success. Their reality can be your reality because whatever is possible for them also is possible for you. Bless them and you will be blessed. Respect and be patient with your personal journey to success.
Worrying excessively	When you find yourself worrying, tell yourself, "Worrying is not going to solve this problem.

excessively	Let me do something "now" that will solve the problem." Then proceed to think - then do something positive to resolve the problem. Focus on being successful today, and tomorrow will take care of itself.
Keeping up with the Joneses	You must come to the realization that nothing you can purchase is worth more than your health or peace of mind, nothing is going to ultimately satisfy or complete you, and nothing will impress you more than you being comfortable with yourself. You don't need external props to hold you up.
Addictions	When you start to feel a strong craving for something unhealthy in order to make yourself feel relaxed or good, have the following conversation with yourself. Eventually, you will realize that you are worth more than the addiction. Memorize the following: Is this going to ultimately satisfy me? No. Is this how I want to live my life? No. Is this worth me losing my life? No. What do I really want? Love. Do I want to destroy myself? No. I really want to love, respect and appreciate myself more. This will bring me ultimate satisfaction.
Procrastination	Make the task fun. Put some good music on, recite positive affirmations to yourself, relax in the process and don't procrastinate on it, "Just do it!"

Need for romantic relationship	Realize that a romantic relationship is not going to complete you. Next, develop a stronger relationship with yourself by loving, respecting and appreciating yourself more. This will make you feel and look good from the inside out. Ultimately, you will find people that are attracted to people who are complete within themselves.
The Gossip Circle	Each time you are confronted with this situation, affirm to yourself: "I don't have the time or energy to waste on things or people that are not positive or productive in life."

What Do You Think? Notes, Comments, Commitments:

_____
_____
_____
_____
_____
_____
_____
_____

You Are Powerful Beyond Measure

You are the Greatest
You Feel Great
You Look Great
You Are Great

You are the Greatest.
You may not fully see it now; however, it is there. As you begin to peel back the layers of your barriers, I guarantee you will see your greatness. You will see that you are the love, joy, peace and prosperity that you seek outside of yourself. At this point, you will begin achieving your external goals. Make a decision to live every moment in a conscious pursuit of operating at your next level of power.

You are Powerful.
Within you is the power to overcome any obstacle that stands in your way of authentic success. This inner power will give you boundless energy, and enduring strength to create the life you desire.

You are Intelligent.
All the knowledge you will ever need exists within you right now. There may be times when you feel like you do not know what you

are doing. Don't worry! Your human intellect is getting caught up in the details. Relax your mind! This will allow your divine intelligence to figure out the details and reveal the right answers to you. You have the intelligence to create and orchestrate greatness in your life.

You are Courageous.
Fear is a negative emotion that you have complete control over. The power that is within you gives you the courage to face any difficulty with boldness and confidence. You are able to conquer all of your fears and keep moving forward to achieve authentic success.

You are Unique.
You are not a Xerox copy. You are a unique individual expression of love. Appreciate your uniqueness and flaunt it with style and grace.

You are Beautiful.
You possess an inner spirit of love that radiates through all that you do, and all that you are. For this reason, you look magnificent. You are attractive and you handle negative people and situations with love and power.

You are Rich.
Your wealth is the love, joy and peace that is within you. Visualize in your mind a clear picture of the riches you desire. As you begin to tap into your inner resources, you will manifest the external riches you desire.

You are Organized and Prepared.
Divine order rules your life. As you begin mentally preparing yourself via self-empowerment, you will take daily steps to be organized, prepared and equipped to handle life's challenges.

You are disciplined.

You have the power of discipline within you. As you become more focused, your discipline skills will grow. As a result, you will find yourself being more consistent with fulfilling your purpose and doing the daily work required to accomplish your ultimate goals.

What Do You Think? Notes, Comments, Commitments:

_____

_____

_____

_____

_____

_____

_____

_____

What Do You Think? Notes, Comments, Commitments:

_____

_____

_____

_____

_____

_____

_____

_____

Empower Yourself To Produce Powerful Results

Self-Empowerment

Self-Empowerment means to give myself the power to fulfill my purpose, achieve my personal and professional goals, overcoming all my life challenges to achieve happiness and authentic success. Authentic success is defined as the experience of more love, joy, peace and prosperity in the now.

5 Self-Empowerment Characteristics

1. I take full responsibility for my happiness and success

2. I Love myself and I have great value and self-worth

3. I Believe in myself and in my ability to succeed

4. I Present and Communicate myself in a loving and powerful manner

5. I am a powerful, effective team player

5 Self-Empowerment Characteristics

1. ***I am an Empowered person who takes full responsibility for my happiness and success.*** I do not depend on people or situations to make me happy or successful. I am the love, joy, peace and prosperity that I seek. Therefore, I now attract and draw to myself all that I need and want to make myself happy and successful. Even in difficult times.

2. ***I am an Empowered person. I love myself and I have great value and self-worth.*** Daily, I love myself by nurturing and developing my mind, body and spirit. I have great value and self-worth because I know who I am, I know my purpose and I have great services to offer in my personal and professional life. Therefore, I do not depend on people, my position or material things to give me value and self-worth. My great value and self-worth comes from my ability to put excellent into everything that I do, both personally and professionally.

3. ***I am an Empowered person. I believe in myself and in my ability to succeed.*** I am powerful enough to succeed in life. I trust and have confidence in a higher power within me to overcome challenges, fulfill my purpose and to achieve my deepest goals and desires. I am my own cheerleader.

4. ***I am an Empowered person. I present and communicate myself in a loving and powerful manner.*** I have a positive attitude and self-image. I radiate peace and power. Moreover, I communicate effectively with all people and I have no problem getting what I want from the world.

5. ***I am an Empowered person. I am a powerful, effective team player.*** I have the emotional fortitude to be open to whatever information I need to hear in order to succeed. I accept constructive criticism and points of view that are the opposite of mine and I deal powerfully with all conflicts.

3 Powerful Self-Empowerment Techniques for Personal Growth & Development

1. I Meditate

2. I Affirm My Power via Self-Talk

3. I Visualize My Goals and Desires via Mental Imagery

Self-Empowerment Technique #1:

I Meditate

Meditation - To relax and center my mind, body and spirit. To surrender to a higher power greater than myself.

I will take time each day for quiet reflection. I will be still and let my body relax and let my mind be free of all negative thoughts, beliefs and concepts. I will focus on love, joy, peace and prosperity because this is what I ultimately desire to create in my life. Not just for myself but all the people on the planet.

Meditation will allow me to:
1. Tap into my higher power
2. Listen to my intuition
3. Get in alignment with what the universe has for me

1. Meditation allows me to tap into my higher power. When I am faced with negative challenges and I do not think I can overcome them, my *higher power* will assist me in overcoming the challenges. My higher power is powerful enough to heal and transform any negative challenge into a positive opportunity. Even when I do not think that I can achieve this goal, there is a higher power within me that can. I am learning to trust and believe in my higher power more and more. This gives me great confidence.

2. Meditation allows me to listen to my intuition. My intuition helps me to make effective decisions in my daily life. It allows me to react & respond to challenging situations in a powerful manner. Intuition helps me to see people for who they really are. This helps me to not allow negative people or situations to drain my energy or take me off focus. My intuition is always speaking to me and I really am beginning to pay attention to this powerful inner voice. It saves me a lot of time and energy when making decisions.

3. Meditation puts me in alignment with who I am, my purpose, desires and talents. This surpasses all outside negative conditioning, people and situations. When my identity, purpose, desires and talents are revealed from within, nothing or no one can stop me from executing what I have come to this planet to accomplish.

The benefits I receive from my meditation:
1. It keeps me off drugs, alcohol and other negative addictions
2. It re-energizes and renews my physical mind, body and spirit.
3. It reduces my stress and anxiety.
4. It lowers blood pressure.
5. It reduces my headache and bodily pain.
6. It allows me to sleep peacefully through the night.
7. It helps me to be a more physically, emotionally, and spiritually powerful person.

Self-Empowerment Technique #2:

I Affirm My Power via Self-Talk "The Power of Words"

Affirmations/Self-Talk - Positive Affirmations are powerful words, thoughts or ideas that are aimed at producing a desired result. "I am Powerful. I Am Intelligent. I Am Courageous. I Am Beautiful." Positive affirmations reflect and dominate my inner conversation with my inner self.

Positive affirmations allow me to:
1. Regain my power
2. Transform negativity into something positive
3. Open my mind to possibility thinking
4. Develop and reinforce good habits and behaviors

1. Affirmations allow me to regain my power – When I am feeling fearful, doubtful or insecure and need emotional support, affirming, "I am Powerful, I Am Intelligent, I Am Courageous." allows me to regain my power. Affirming my power as often as possible makes me believe and have confidence in my ability to do what I say that I am going to do. At this level of empowerment, I feel better and when I feel better – I produce better results in my life. Moreover, affirming my power energizes me to transcend all negative conditioning to be the powerful person I need to be in order to overcome life challenges to succeed in life. At this level of empowerment, I can be, do and create anything that my heart desires.

2. Affirmations allow me to transform negativity into something positive - When I am confronted with negativity; I have the power to transform that negativity into something positive. Now, I realize that it is my inner thoughts that create my reality. If my intention is to be successful, then I must focus my thoughts on the positive, regardless of negative appearances. This does not mean to ignore the negative; however, when I focus my thoughts on the positive, eventually, the positive will outweigh the negative. At this level of empowerment, I will produce positive results in my life, because this is a universal law.

3. Affirmations allow me to open my mind to my greatest potential and possibility – When I speak the words, "I am Powerful and I am Intelligent," I am sending a powerful message to my brain to produce powerful results. When my mind is open to my highest potential and possibility, it allows me to think beyond negative appearances - to realize powerful solutions and produce powerful results. This allows me to tap into a higher power and intelligence greater than myself in order to succeed. At this level of empowerment, I will realize my highest potential and possibility - not just for myself, but for all the people on this planet.

4. Affirmations allow me to reinforce good habits and behaviors - Affirming, "I am the presence and the power of love." reinforces good habits and behaviors that support me in materializing the love, joy, peace and prosperity that I truly desire and deserve. This will also allow me to be consciously aware of when I am not performing at my highest potential. The more I affirm my power, the more control I have over developing good habits and behaviors that support real authentic power and success.

The Benefits I receive from affirmations are:
- o It helps me to believe in myself and in my ability to be successful
- o It opens my mind to possibilities that I had not thought of

- o It re-enforces the importance of developing good habits and behaviors
- o It allows me to put things in the right perspective
- o It helps me to feel better mentally and emotionally
- o It allows me to gain control over my negative emotions and feelings
- o It allows me to take back the power that I have given to negative situations or people
- o It renews my mind, body and spirit so that I am able to be more powerful in the world.

What Do You Think? Notes, Comments, Commitments:

_____

_____

_____

_____

_____

_____

_____

_____

What Do You Think? Notes, Comments, Commitments:

_____

_____

_____

_____

Self-Empowerment Technique **#3:**

I Visualize My Goals and Desires via Mental

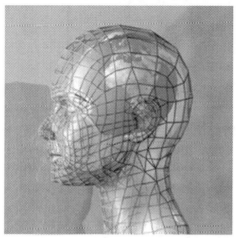

Imagery

Visualization – Having a clear mental picture in my mind, body and spirit of who I desire to be and what I desire to create.

As often as I can, I will close my eyes and visualize myself doing, being and accomplishing my highest potential and possibility.

I will maintain a clear mental picture of my goals and the steps necessary to achieve them. Then, I will mentally rehearse them. Ultimately, I will discover the power within to create what is in my heart to create. At this level of awareness, I am motivated and energized to accomplish anything I desire to accomplish. Moreover, visualization will prepare me to take full advantage of life's greatest opportunities.

Benefits of Visualization:

1. Visualization allows me to create a powerful new self-image and lifestyle
2. Visualization allows me to develop my belief and confidence in my higher potential and possibility
3. Visualization allows me to give powerful performances every time

1. **Visualization allows me to create a powerful new self-image and lifestyle -** If my intention is to be successful, then I must have a powerful self-image and lifestyle. I can achieve this by visualizing myself being a powerful person and having a rich lifestyle. I will not allow my logical mind to discourage me because if I can clearly visualize it, I can achieve it. This will allow me to tap into a higher power within myself in order to orchestrate and engineer my greatest potential and possibilities.

2. **Visualization allows me to develop my belief and confidence in my higher potential and possibility -** Before I can manifest my desires, I must believe in my ability to achieve them. Visualization forces me to use my imagination to stimulate my feelings and emotions into powerful beliefs. These powerful beliefs will empower my ability to do anything I put my mind to. At this point, I can go out into the world and create and produce anything I truly desire in my life.

3. **Visualization allows me to give a powerful performance every time -** If my intention is to be successful, then I must always give a powerful performance; be it in front of one person or twenty million people. I must constantly visualize myself being the powerful person I know that I can be. Rehearsing my performance in my mind gives me the self-confidence I need to give a great performance every time.

Tips for Creative Visualization:

1. If you have trouble getting a clear mental picture, try cutting out pictures from books, magazines and catalogs. Whenever you see a picture that you are attracted to or that inspires you, cut it out. You may want to create a collage with pictures that really inspire you. Next, put your collage of pictures in a place where you can see it as often as possible. This will dramatically help you to get a clear mental picture in your mind of what you desire.

2. You can increase the benefits of visualization by reciting positive affirmations while looking at the pictures. As you are looking at the pictures, say to yourself, "I am powerful enough to achieve this in my life." This will help to increase your chances of attracting and drawing to yourself exactly what you need in order to materialize your deepest goals and desires.

3. To get the maximum benefit out of these visualization techniques, you should visualize once upon getting up in the morning, throughout the day and once just before going to sleep at night. Doing these visualization exercises consistently will assist you in staying motivated, focused, and conscious of who you desire to be and what you desire to create in your life.

What Do You Think? Notes, Comments, Commitments:

_____
_____
_____
_____
_____
_____
_____

Do The Inner Work Required for Success Now

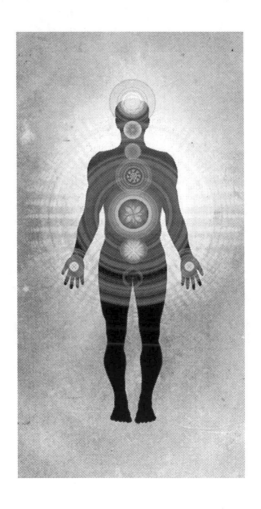

Affirm: I Am The Presence and the Power of Love

I Love Myself Unconditionally – My love for myself is not regulated by my successes, failures or who likes me or not. I love myself unconditionally because I am unconditional love. At this level of empowerment I attract and draw to myself the love, joy, peace and great riches I truly desire and deserve.

I Am Responsible for My Life – I take full responsibility for healing and transforming my life to achieve my personal and professional goals and desires.

I Am Perfect Health – Every bone, muscle, tissue and cell of my body is filled with love and perfection. Therefore, I am eternally youthful, beautiful and in perfect health.

I Am Forgiving – I forgive myself and other people for any wrongdoings; therefore, I am free from guilt, shame and resentment. I have learned the lesson and now I am prepared to go to my next level of love, joy, peace and prosperity.

I Am Standing on Solid Ground – I am powerful enough to stop allowing negative people, situations and circumstances to have power and control over me. Therefore, there is nothing or no one that can stop me from loving, believing and having confidence in myself.

I Only Have Loving Relationships With Everyone (Family, Friends, Enemies, The World) - I love, respect and appreciate myself; therefore, I treat everyone with love and respect. I no longer feel the need to please people or understand why they do what they do. I accept people for who they are because I know who I Am. I give Love. I give Love. I give Love.

I Am Living my Life On Purpose – My main purpose is to discover how profoundly powerful I am to create Love, Joy, Peace and Great Riches in this world.

I Am Free, Free, Free – I am free because I know who I am, and I know that I can do all things with love that supports and strengthens me. Now, I operate at my fullest potential to achieve my personal and professional goals and desires.

In the name of Love, I am Love and I am willing to see and experience Love in this world.

The Power of Self-Love

Philosophers, psychologists, medical doctors, and motivation gurus agree that Love is the most powerful force on earth. The human mind cannot possibly understand, intellectualize, or limit the power of love. Love is so powerful and infinite that it is synonymous with only one other word: God. God is love and you are an expression of that love. The desire to express this love is part of your being, so fundamentally woven into your essence that you cannot be separated from it. It can be suppressed or denied, but never extinguished. Love is so powerful that it is patient - until you choose to tap into its power.   If your intention is to achieve success now, start by tapping into the power of love within you. You can achieve this by learning to love yourself via self-empowerment.

Self-love is not about being vain or perfect. Self-love is about being authentic, regardless of the challenges you may face. It allows you to peel back the layers of your life and discover your most authentic self. It is an awesome way of existing in the world. It also entails certain actions, like flowing with life rather than against it; moving toward conscious living rather than unconscious living; treating facts with respect rather than living in denial; acting responsibly rather than irresponsibly. Self-love creates a confidence in your ability to think, learn, and make effective decisions. It helps you to react and respond to negative situations and people in a powerful way. Self-love is the basic ingredient for true happiness and success "now."

Remember, Loving yourself does not just require accumulating more things, people or accomplishments. It requires that you seek the truth about Love from within you. This concept will revolutionize your life and take you to your next level of authentic success.

What Do You Think? Notes, Comments, Commitments:

_____

_____

_____

_____

_____

_____

_____

_____

-

_____

_____

Self-Love Evaluation

Answer the following 10 questions, Yes or No. Remember, only you can ask and answer these questions for yourself. Be honest with yourself for powerful results.

1. **Y/N** **Now, when asked, "Who is the most important person in my life?" do I answer "myself"?**

2. **Y/N** **Now, am I nurturing my mind, body and spirit on a daily basis?**

3. **Y/N** **Now, have I stopped allowing negative things and people to control me by draining my energy and taking me off focus?**

4. **Y/N** **Now, I Have I forgiven myself for any mistakes or bad decisions that I have made?**

5. **Y/N** **Now, am I treating everyone with love and respect?**

6. **Y/N** **Now, do I acknowledge and confront my internal barriers, energy drainers and addictions?**

7. **Y/N** **Now, am I creating success based on what I authentically desire for my life?**

8. **Y/N** **Now, do I feel like I am a beautiful person?**

9. **Y/N** **Now, have I stopped depending on external props to make me feel secure within myself?**

10. **Y/N** **Now, am I sensitive to my internal needs (love and attention) and am I fulfilling those needs in a way that supports self-love?**

Add up your number of "Yes" responses and write down the number: #_____

Add up your number of "No" responses and write down the number: #_____

If you have 8 or more "Yes" responses:

- o You love yourself and are on your way to a healthy, bright and exciting future.
- o However, don't forget that loving yourself is a daily process and you must continue to empower yourself to love yourself even more.
- o Remember, there is always a next level in the evolution of "love" to evolve to and you must continue to keep moving forward.
- o Do not allow other people to make you feel guilty because they perceive self-love as being self-centered. The more you love yourself, the easer it is to allow other people to love themselves.

If you have 3 or more "no" responses:
- o You don't love yourself as much as you should or could. If you are hurt or disappointed by your score, don't be. This is not a bad thing. It just means that you must work on loving yourself more. Remember, if you are not open to your own truth, you may find yourself falling deeper into self-destruction and a dead end future.
- o They say, "Knowledge is power." However, knowledge is only potential power, because if you don't use the information/results from your self-evaluation, then the knowledge will not be powerful to you. Use this information to re-evaluate your desires, acknowledge root barriers and

commit to empower yourself to overcome your life challenges to achieve your goals. Remember, regardless of the challenges in your life, you have the power to transform every situation from a negative to a positive one.

o One of the first questions I ask my audiences is, "Do you love, respect and appreciate yourself?" In most cases, 95% says, "Yes". However, after completing our self-love test, they realize that they do not love, respect and appreciate themselves as much as they thought. One of the major reasons people do not succeed in living a better life is that they are in denial. Denial means to refuse to admit the truth about the root of your problems. The root of their problems usually stem from their inability to love, and believe in themselves. People who live in a state of denial, in most cases, live their lives blaming people or situations for the reason they do not love themselves and cannot be happy or successful. As long as there is something or someone "out there" to pin their dissatisfaction and failures on, they never have to face themselves.

o The Big Void – If you have a big void in your life and have not found anything satisfactory to fill it, you may want to fill it with the power of self-love. I guarantee that you will fill the void.

o Do not procrastinate. Do not wait until you get a new job, relationship, house or car to love yourself. Love yourself today.

The Power of Self-Love

10 Tips for Improving Your Next Self-Love Evaluation

1. _____ **When asked who is the most important person in your life, do you answer "myself"?** "No, my children, (or spouse, or friends) are." When you are the most important person, you naturally nurture and develop your mind, body and spirit, which ultimately empowers' you to operate at your fullest potential. When you are solid and strong within yourself, then you 1) fulfill your purpose and materialize your goals and desires and 2) you inspire and help other people to fulfill their purpose and achieve their goals and desires.

2. _____ **Am I nurturing my mind, body and spirit on a daily basis?** "No. I just don't have the time." Your mind, body and spirit are your most important and valuable resources to you achieving a successful life. In order for you to overcome your life challenges to achieve the life you desire, you must possess a strong mind, body and spirit. Learn to make the time to nurture your mind, body and spirit. You will be so glad you did.

3.   ___ **Have I stopped allowing negative people, situations and circumstances to drain my energy and block me from completing my daily objectives?** "No, because I feel too overwhelmed." Please realize, without a sufficient amount of energy, it is almost impossible to complete your daily objectives. When you stop allowing your energy to be drained, you will find it much easier to "do what you must do" to overcome life challenges to complete daily objectives. No excuses.

4.   ___ **Have I forgiven myself for any mistakes or bad decisions that I have made?** "No." Not forgiving yourself is an energy drainer that makes it difficult to attract love, joy, peace and riches into your life. Why? Because, you will not believe that you are worthy of it. Please realize that we will all make mistakes in our process of growth and development. So forgive yourself and do not give your mistakes or bad decisions any more thought or energy. The key to forgiving yourself is to learn the lesson and *re-focus on a higher vision for your life.*

5.   ___ **Am I treating everyone with love and respect?** "No, because they do not treat me with love and respect." In most cases they are treating you like you treat yourself. The relationships we have with other people, usually, reflect the relationship we have with ourselves. Treat yourself with love and respect and people will eventually treat you with love and respect - regardless of their past behavior.

6.   ___ **Now, do I acknowledge and confront my internal barriers, energy drainers and addictions?** "No, because I have too many other things on my plate to deal with first." Please realize, those things that are on your plate will always be there - in one form or another. If your intention is to

succeed in life, then you must first resolve your internal barriers, **energy drainers and addictions**. This will set you free to realize your true power to accomplish any goal that you set for yourself.

7. _____ **Am I creating success based on what I authentically desire for my life?** "No, because the world's definition of success is different from mine." Which definition do you think will bring you the greatest satisfaction? Remember, building success based on other people's definition of success is like building your empire on sand. It would only take a strong wind to destroy in seconds what you took years to build. Building success based on your internal definition of success is like building your empire on solid ground. When you build your success on solid ground, nothing or no one can destroy it, not even you.

8. _____ **Do I feel like I am a beautiful person?** "No, because I do not look like the people on television or in the magazines." Always remember you have a unique beauty that radiates from the essence of your being, if you allow it to. Re-Focus on exercising your inner beauty, regardless of your physical appearance. This will empower you to radiate your true authentic beauty. Moreover, this authentic beauty will be reflected in your self-esteem, attitude, confidence level, self-image and reaction and response to life.

9. _____ **Now, have I stopped depending on external props to make me feel secure within myself?** "No." Please realize - evaluating your level of self-worth and value based on what you have or don't have is self-destructive and dis-empowering. If it is your intent to increase your level of self-worth and value to achieve the life you desire, then re-focus on operating at your fullest potential at every given moment. This will allow you

to develop the confidence and security within yourself to overcome any life challenge to fulfill your purpose and achieve your deepest goals and desires.

10. ___ **Am I sensitive to my internal needs (love and attention) and am I fulfilling those needs in a way that supports self-love?** "No, because I am still dependent on other people to take care of my internal needs." A lot of time and energy can be spent manipulating other people to fulfill your internal needs. This is an energy drainer that can prevent you from moving to your next level of success. Moreover, eventually people are going to get tired of taking care of you. So get the lesson now, start fulfilling your own internal needs. Ultimately, this will set you free to create the life that you authentically desire.

What Do You Think? Notes, Comments, Commitments:

_____

_____

_____

_____

_____

_____

_____

_____

Affirm: I Am The Greatest

**I Feel Great
I Look Great
I Am Great**

I Am Powerful – I am spiritually, mentally and physically strong enough to overcome my life challenges to achieve my goals and desires. I am powerful enough to fulfill my purpose and achieve the love, joy, peace and great riches I truly desire and deserve!

I Am Intelligent – I have the brainpower to create, orchestrate and manifest greatness in my life. I learn and master any information or skill because I am a thinker and I use my brain to think. My mind is strong enough to visualize and manifest anything that my heart desires.

I Am Courageous – I fear nothing or no one. I am the presence and the power of love. Love is the most powerful force on earth. Therefore, I am powerful enough to overcome my fears, doubts and insecurities to achieve my heart's desires. I can do all things with love that supports and strengthens me.

I Am Unique – I am a special individual expression of love. Only I can do things the way that I do them. I add something extra special to this world.

I Am Beautiful – I am beautiful because I am the Presence and the Power of Love.

I Am The Greatest!

I Feel Great! I Look Great! I Am Great!

I Give Thanks!

Do You Believe In Yourself?

Believing In Yourself – Self-Evaluation
For each of the following questions, answer Yes or No:

1. <u>Y / N</u> Now, do I have an internal "knowing"/Belief that regardless of the challenges I now face – I will prevail in the end, not weakened but stronger? (Regardless of what people think or believe.)

2. <u>Y / N</u> Now, when negativity starts to attack me and I start doubting myself, do I immediately surrender to my higher power? (Regardless of where I am.)

3. <u>Y / N</u> Now, am I maintaining a clear mental picture in my mind of my goals and who I need to be in order to achieve those goals? (Regardless of present appearances.)

4. <u>Y / N</u> Now, am I presenting and communicating myself confidently – with a powerful self-image that reflects my deepest goals and desires? (Regardless of people, situations or circumstances.)

5. <u>Y / N</u> Now, am I reacting and responding to life's challenges in a powerful manner? Meaning, have *I stopped allowing* negativity to: 1) drain my energy and destroy my spirit, 2) make me feel angry, fearful, frustrated and insecure, or 3) stop me from fulfilling my purpose and accomplishing my goals?

Add up your number of "Yes" responses and write down the number #_____.

Add up your number of "No" responses and write down the number #_____.

If you have 4 or more "Yes" responses:
- ❖ You believe in yourself and are on your way to a bright and exciting future.
- ❖ Don't forget that believing in yourself is a daily process and you must continue to develop a higher belief in your abilities.
- ❖ Push yourself to new levels of believing in your ability by setting higher goals for yourself.
- ❖ Assist other people in believing in themselves by reaffirming their power.

If you have 2 or more "No" responses:
- ❖ You don't believe in yourself as much as you should or could. If you ignore this revelation, you may find yourself overcome by self-destructive habits and a dead-end future.

- ❖ If you are hurt or disappointed by your score, don't be. Use this information to empower yourself to gain control over your belief in yourself.

- ❖ Remember, if you don't believe in yourself – this is not a death sentence. If you ignore this information – it is a death sentence. Start the process of believing in the power within you. It will transform your life.

What Do You Think? Notes, Comments, Commitments:

_____
_____
_____
_____
_____
_____
_____
_____

What Do You Think? Notes, Comments, Commitments:

_____
_____
_____
_____
_____
_____
_____
_____

5 Tips to Improve Your next "Believe In Yourself" Evaluation

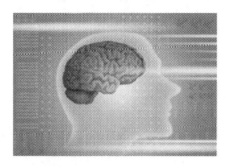

1. ___ **Do I have an internal "knowing" that regardless of the challenges I now face – I will prevail in the end, not weakened but stronger?** (Despite what other people think or believe.) "No." If you are reacting to your challenges negatively, it means that you are fearful that you are not going to succeed in the end. Make it a ritual to surrender to your higher power via self-empowerment. Ultimately, this is how you develop an inner "Belief" or "Knowing" that you will prevail in the end, not weakened but stronger.

2. ___ **When negativity starts to attack me and I start doubting myself, do I immediately surrender to my higher power?** (Regardless of where I am physically.) "No." Remember, at every level of success there will be negative attacks; learn to react to them powerfully. Make it a ritual, when you are under attack, to immediately start to re-affirm your power. Repeat to yourself, "I am powerful beyond measure. I will not allow this attacker to destroy or keep me from accomplishing my goals." Ultimately you will discover the power within to overcome the negative attacks in order to keep moving your life forward.

3. ___ **Am I maintaining a clear mental picture in my mind of my goals and who I must be in order to accomplish those goals?** (Regardless of present appearances.) "No." Remember,

negative appearances will keep you from focusing on your highest potential and possibility. Don't fall in to this trap. As often as possible, close your eyes and see yourself being a powerful person and having exactly what you desire. Eventually, negative appearances will fall away and you will manifest your desires in your physical world.

4. ___ **Am I presenting and communicating myself confidently – with a powerful self-image?** (Regardless of what I have or don't have.) "No, because I do not have what I need physically to present myself powerfully." Remember, your presentation and communication skills are key elements to getting what you desire from people. Make it a ritual to practice your presentation and communication skills 24/7. This will allow you to develop a powerful self-image. At this point, you can go out into the world and powerfully get whatever you desire.

5. ___ **Now, am I reacting and responding to life's challenges in a powerful manner?** "No. Well it depends on the life challenge." Hear this loud and clear, No, it does not depend on the life challenge. If it is your intent to succeed in life, then you must make a conscious decision to react and respond to every life challenge powerfully. Accepting this concept will allow you to perceive every life challenge as an opportunity to discover how profoundly powerful you are. Remember, practice makes perfect. The more proficient you become at reacting and responding to life challenges powerfully, the easier it will be for you to fulfill your purpose and materialize your deepest goals and desires.

Internalizing these simple but powerful concepts for loving and believing in yourself will allow you to discover what you need to do in order to fulfill your purpose and achieve your deepest goals and desires.

In addition, these Success Principles are what trigger your **SUCCESS MECHANISMS** and you start to feel SUCCESS:

Success – Your success stems from you and only you. It is not dependent on what you have or do not have or whether people like you or not. When you feel successful, you react and respond to life successfully. At this level, you are open and receptive to an unlimited amount of success to flow into your life.

Understanding – Your understanding stems from your "knowing" who you are and the source of your supply. You are the power of Love and your supply comes from a higher power within you. Therefore, you attract positive opportunities and people that support you in becoming successful.

Courage – Your courage stems from the power of love within you to conquer all your fears and life challenges. When you exercise courage, you can do anything you put your mind to. This allows to you to create the successful life you truly desire and deserve.

Change – Your ability to change/transform allows you to make the necessary adjustments, internal and external, in your life that leads to success.

Established - The more established you feel within yourself, the easier it is for you to materialize your goals and desires in the face of life challenges.

Security - Your sense of security will stem from your understanding that you are powerful enough to adapt to any environment or person to materialize your goals and desires.

Serenity – Your sense of Serenity will stem from your ability to overcome worry and stress to still operate at your fullest potential to achieve your goals and desires.

BELIEVE In Yourself

To believe means to accept in your mind that something is true or real, often underpinned by an emotional or spiritual sense of certainty/knowing. Belief is a feeling or emotion that motivates us to act, do, or accomplish something.

Believing in you - means to trust and have confidence in a Higher Power within yourself to achieve authentic success.

Ingredients for Believing in Yourself

a. **Trust** - Trust in your ability to succeed. This will give you an inner "knowing" that regardless of the challenges you now face – you will prevail in the end, not weakened but stronger.

b. **Faith** – Have faith in a higher power within you. This will give you the power to overcome any challenges that could keep you from accomplishing your goals.

c. **Hope** – Be optimistic. This will give you a positive attitude in difficult times to keep moving forward, no matter what.

d. **Confidence** – Present and communicate yourself powerfully. This will give you the self-assurance needed to sustain the respect of people around you and to accomplish your goals.

Your beliefs about yourself are evident in the way you react and respond to life. When you say that you believe in yourself, it means that you consistently exercise the power within you to create the life you desire.

Notes:

_____

_____

_____

_____

_____

_____

_____

_____

_____

_____

Empower Your Belief System

1.   ___**Your beliefs translate into powerful feelings and emotions that motivate and control what you THINK, leading to what you do.** Everything that you do stems from your beliefs. Have you ever asked yourself, "Why did I do that?" or, "Why did I react that way?" You may want to look at what you believed the outcome was going to be. Consciously or unconsciously, you did it because you believed it would bring a specific outcome.

2.   ___**Faith and hope fuels your belief system.** To accomplish anything, you must have faith and hope in your ability to achieve it. Have you ever asked yourself the questions, "Why can't I accomplish this goal?" or "Why can't I master this skill?" You may want to look at your belief in your ability to accomplish the goal. Believing in yourself means starting out with nothing except an idea and a vision, then doing the daily work needed to accomplish your goals. This will allow you to build faith and hope within yourself.

3.   ___**Protect your belief system so that you cannot be manipulated into doing things you do not desire to do.** Can you say, "No" to people, without having them manipulate you into saying, "Yes"? If your answer is, "No, I cannot say no to people," then you have a major challenge. If you cannot say 'no' to people and mean it, then you will make it more difficult to accomplish your goals. Why? Because you only have a certain amount of time and energy in any given day. If people are able to manipulate you into doing what they want you to do and dismiss or invalidate what you want, then you cannot focus on your goals. Do not allow people to manipulate you into believing that you are a bad person because you did not do that favor for them. Please note, this does not mean that you cannot do favors for people. Just make sure that 1) it is convenient for you, 2) it does not take away from your goals, and 3) it does not go against what you value and believe in.

4.   ___**Your belief about yourself motivates and inspires other people.** When you believe in yourself, it shows in your energy level and enthusiasm about life. Your self-image and presentation to the world is positive. People are attracted to powerful people who believe in themselves and have positive attitudes and self-images. This is how jobs are secured, promotions are granted, and major sales are made.

5.   ___**Your belief in yourself controls your self-image.** As soon as you walk into a room full of people, you have told everyone what you believe about yourself by the way you present and communicate yourself. When you believe in yourself, it is expressed by your self-confidence, energy and a powerful presents and self-image. This includes the way you walk, talk, dress, communicate and interact with people.

6.   **___You attract to yourself what you believe about yourself.** We are living magnets that attract people, opportunities, material possessions and experiences based on what we believe and think about ourselves. If you have a negative attitude, you will attract negativity into your life. If you have a positive attitude, and are open to the possibilities of life, you will attract positive things, opportunities and people into your life.

What Do You Think? Notes, Comments, Commitments:

_____

_____

_____

_____

_____

_____

_____

_____

What Do You Think? Notes, Comments, Commitments:

_____

_____

_____

_____

_____

I Am Powerful Enough

Master Relationships by Developing a Solid Relationship With Yourself

The only way to have a successful relationship with anyone is to first have a successful relationship with yourself. You must first love, respect and appreciate yourself before you can love anyone else. One of the most damaging mistakes that people make Is looking for love and self-worth outside of themselves before they have found love and self-worth inside of themselves.

If you want to be successful in life, you must first develop love, respect, and appreciation for yourself. There is no getting around this fundamental law. Ninety-five percent of the time we attract to ourselves what we really believe about ourselves. This is very difficult to accept, but nonetheless, it is true. If you are into abusing yourself by feeling ashamed of who you are, then you will attract abusive people. These negative people will verbally and physically abuse and victimize you. On the other hand, if you genuinely love yourself, you will attract people who will support you in love.

8 Tips for Enhancing Your Relationship with Yourself

1. Make a Commitment to spend at least 20 minutes a day with your personal and professional development! You can start by meditating, reviewing your goals, planning a strategy to achieve your goals and empowering yourself with powerful affirmations and visualization exercises. This will allow you to become a stronger, more powerful person in the world.

2. Do the "Amazing Mirror Exercise"
Look at yourself in the mirror and affirm, "I love you." Make eye contact with yourself. This will help you to develop a stronger relationship with yourself. This affirmation also will increase your sense of self-worth and value. Affirming to yourself, "I love you" and internalizing it, will heal and transform your life beyond your wildest dreams.

3. Nurture Yourself
Do not dismiss this exercise as being crazy. By touching yourself, you acknowledge the beautiful body that God has given you. Lovingly touch your face, arms, legs, feet, hands, etc. Even if your body is not what you desire it to be, love it as if it is. Be willing to see the beauty in your body because it is there. Take time to groom and appreciate your physical appearance. It is yours, so you may as well love it with all of your heart. If you do not love your body, how can you expect anyone else to love or appreciate it?

4. Implement a daily exercise program into your life
If you are going to maintain a healthy body you must exercise 3 to 5 days a week. This will help you to be mentally, spiritually and physically stronger. As you increase your strength, you also increase your potential for success.

5. Learn to spend quality time alone

Daily, you must spend time alone doing something that you enjoy. This could be meditating, listening to inspirational music, reading motivational books, thinking and planning for your future, writing in your diary, etc. This will bring you closer to your self. The closer you are to your self, the closer you can get to other people.

6. Be aware of your body language

Always be aware of your body language. Negativity can be reflected in your body language. Your body language must express power and self-confidence at all times. This will allow you to send positive messages to your mind, body and spirit. It doesn't matter what others think. Initially, they probably will say, "Who do you think you are, part of the royal family?" Remember, you do not have to justify yourself personal development process to anyone.

7. Dress in a fashion that fits you

Find a fashion that you love. Don't do it because it is in style or because it brings you a lot of attention. Wear it because you love it and it fits your personality and the direction in which you are moving.

8. Learn to relax

Regardless of what is going on in your life, you must learn to relax. Relaxing will help you to think clearly and give you energy. Relaxation is extremely important for your overall health, relationships, advancement and financial wealth.

Avoid These Relationships Pitfalls

1. Stop being a "People Pleaser"

Do you go to the extreme to please people hoping to be loved and accepted? Always remember, you cannot please people 100% of the time, because – the more they get, the more they want. The more money you give them, the more money they need. They never learn to create money for themselves. The more sympathy you give people, the more drama they create to obtain sympathy. The more energy you give them, the more they will take, and before long, you have lost yourself. You must do things to please your heart and soul. If it pleases others, great, but if it doesn't, you still will continue to grow. When you are living your life based in love and truth, all things will happen for the higher good.

2. Believe people when they show you who they are!

Intuition is always speaking to you. Listen when people tell you, "I am in your life to destroy you by stealing your energy and holding you back," or conversely, "I am in your life to support you in love and assist you in growing and moving forward." Do not waste your time and energy on people who are not interested in growing and moving forward. This concept will save you a lot of time and energy when communicating with people.

3. Stop trying to understand why people do what they do -
People will do and think whatever they want, it is a waste of time to analyze their motives. The only person you truly can understand is yourself. Ultimately, when you understand yourself, you will better understand others. If you really want to help people, help them by being a good example of a loving person, without judgment.

4. Stop defining yourself by the standards of others
Stop defining yourself by the master narrative. The master narrative includes people whom you allow to dictate what beauty, success, and happiness are for you. The master narrative will say: This is beauty, success and happiness. Upon review, you realize that you are not it. Then you go through life unconsciously – feeling and thinking that you are ugly, a failure, and worthless. You must write, produce, and star in your own movie called, "This is my life." In this movie you are love, beautiful, intelligent, successful, and secure within yourself. You become what you think about yourself. It is only logical that you should think very highly of yourself. You must look beyond your negative flaws and focus on your positive attributes. Define your own level of success and happiness.

5. Don't mistake the fantasy for the reality
You see someone that you are extremely attracted to; you start to hyperventilate because they are walking in your direction. "Hello, can I take you to dinner?" they ask. You take a deep breath and smile, "Yes, I would love to." You love birds go to dinner at one of the finest restaurants. This person is affectionate and attentive to your every need. They ask, "Do you want to spend the night at my house, because I think I love you?" You say, "Well…yes." It was a night of passion and excitement. You arrive home the next morning around nine o'clock feeling like you have found "the one." Your heart sings, "I am going to the chapel and I am going to get married." You call all your friends telling them about your extraordinary night. Now, it is 1:00 p.m. and you just need to hear their voice, so you call. Instead of hearing their voice, you hear, "I am sorry but this number is not in service." You try again and

again. Now, you are feeling hurt, betrayed and confused. Did they make you feel special just because they wanted sex? Were you so consumed with your fantasy that you could not see what was really going on? Was the night worth the hurt and pain that you feel? Are you now scared by this event? In the future, will you separate the truth from fantasy?

6. Are you an extra in your own life? Don't be!

Are you attending to the needs of family and friends before taking care of your own needs? When you value "self," you intuitively and naturally take better care of yourself. You are a stronger, healthier, more confident person and you become a positive inspiration to everyone around you. This puts you in a better position to uplift other people. In addition, by loving and valuing yourself, you are teaching people how to love and value themselves.

7. Do not allow people to make you angry

Their negative disposition has nothing to do with you, and everything to do with how they feel about themselves. People are usually rude and disrespectful for the following reasons:

> ➢ They want to get your attention but do not know the proper way to do so.
> ➢ They are angry with themselves because they are not where they want to be in life.
> ➢ They are jealous and envious because you are happy and feeling confident about yourself.
> ➢ They have an insatiable need to feel superior by belittling you or other people.

Remember, people do not have any real power or control over you unless - you give it to them. Do not allow people to make you angry, your life is so much bigger than that.

The next time you are confronted with a negative person, learn to tell them directly, "_____ you are not going to disrupted my life or take me off focus with your negative drama. I have a purpose and a dream that I am working on." And move on.

8. Do not create relationships based upon selfish desires

Do not seek to befriend people for what they can do for you, i.e. how much money they have and the company they keep. This will only weaken you in the end. Focus instead on creating your highest potential and possibility and how you can enhance the lives of people around you. You do not need someone else's life, money or friends when you have your own. Befriend people who have a good energy and spirit and because they are moving in the same direction as you are.

9. Learn to Let people go gracefully

Many people get stuck in unproductive relationships because they can't let go. They fear that they will not be able to find love again or attract a better job. When you are a loving, powerful person, you will always attract love and great employment opportunities into your life. Learn to let people go gracefully, so you may open yourself up to new and exciting possibilities and opportunities.

10. Possession is Poison "I own you!"

Possessiveness can end good relationships before they blossom. The attitude of the possessor: I own you; you cannot have any friends I do not approve of; you cannot be attracted to other people or do any activities without me; you must do what I want you to do, when I want you to do it. The person being possessed feels special – for about five minutes. After five minutes, they are left feeling confined, controlled and unhappy. Next, they stop complying with the "ownership agreement." Now, the "owner" feels incomplete and off-balance, so they react with jealousy, manipulation and resort to bullying. At this point, the relationship is moving backwards and each person's level of self-awareness will determine whether they will grow or be destroyed by this communication breakdown.

11. Don't waste your time or energy worrying or complaining if someone else is getting more than you. This will only steal your energy and de-motivate / dis-empower you. You must stay focused on reaching your highest potential and ultimately you will get exactly what you desire. Be patient!

What Do You Think? Notes, Comments, Commitments:

_____
_____
_____
_____
_____

What Do You Think? Notes, Comments, Commitments:

_____
_____
_____
_____
_____
_____
_____
_____

What Do You Think? Notes, Comments, Commitments:

_____
_____
_____

The Center For Mind & Esteem Development, Inc.

You, Inc.

For Professional Advancement

- Leadership
- Self-Management
- Professionalism
- Quality Service
- Team Building

by Marvin Mack
Your Professional Development Coach

BONUS Membership Website: iampowerfulenough.com
Download Additional Self-Help eBooks,
Audios & Videos FREE

Your Virtual Online Training Courses

Table of Contents

Introduction

PPD for Six Sigma will dramatically increase momentum, performance, productivity, customer service and the overall success of your organization.

> *Six Sigma is not merely a quality initiative; it is a Business initiative. Achieving the goal of Six Sigma requires more than small, incremental improvements; it requires breakthroughs in every area of an operation. In statistical terms, "reaching Six Sigma" means that your process or product will perform with almost no defects. Six Sigma is a Total Commitment to and philosophy of excellence, customer focus, process improvement, and the rules of measurement rather than gut feeling. Six Sigma is about making every area of the organization better able to meet the changing needs of customers, markets, and technologies - with benefits for employees, customers, and shareholders.*
> **What is Six Sigma? by Pete Pande and Larry Holpp / The McGraw-Hill Companies, Inc.**

In light of the Six Sigma concept, if your intention is to advance professionally and assist your organization in providing great service and successfully achieving its next level goals and objectives, I highly recommend that you incorporate a PPD component into your daily life for growth and development. It serves to evaluate your strengths and weaknesses. Moreover, PPD provides the empowerment information you need to build on your strengths and correct your weaknesses. It will allow you to develop critical thinking, emotional fortitude and the power consciousness necessary to make changes, take action and achieve next level goals and objectives. This component starts the process of creating a culture of people who are empowered to "Execute" without excuses.

The concept "Lead" consists of 5 Leadership Principles. These principles are designed to assist you in making effective decisions in your personal and professional life that lead to giving great service and the accomplishment of your goals and objectives. Moreover, these leadership principles will serve as reminder of how to overcome your daily challenges to achieve positive results.

Our goal is to share some information with you that will allow you to:

- Clarify and Confirm your professional goals and objectives
- Implement a growth and development strategy
- Take Action Now
- Focus your time, energy and thoughts on being powerful and productive
- Develop the mentality to overcome daily challenges to achieve objectives to your ultimate goals
- Eliminate energy drainers from blocking your success and much more.

Your objective is to review the information, take what you can use to empower yourself, and leave the rest alone. Is it your deepest intent to achieve your personal and professional goals and objectives? If so, make it a ritual to practice these 5 Leaderships Principles. This will empower you to discover the power within to provide great service and realize your ultimate goals and desires.

I recommend that you re-affirm the 5 Leadership Principles to yourself 3 or more times a day. This will empower you to re-focus your time, energy, and thoughts on being powerful and productive. At this level of empowerment, you will make a series of good decisions that support your ultimate goals and desires, no matter what.

The Center For Mind & Esteem Development, Inc.
Self-Evaluation for
Presentation & Communication Skills

Name: ....

Date: ....

Score: ....

Evaluate yourself based on your current performance, relative to some of the great presenters and communicators of our time.

Level 1	Level 2	Level 3	Level 4	Level 5 Leader
Unsatisfactory	Below Standard	Meets Standard	Above Standard	Outstanding Leader

1. Am I presenting A Powerful Self-Image?	1	2	3	4	5

2. Am I articulating my words with knowledge, energy, and authority?	1	2	3	4	5

3. Am I communicating with all people effectively?	1	2	3	4	5

4. Am I dressed for Success on a daily basis?	1	2	3	4	5

5. Am I getting what I need from people, both personally and professionally?	1	2	3	4	5

Add up all your score for an Overall Total ....

The Center For Mind & Esteem Development, Inc.
Self-Evaluation for
Professional Advancement

Your Next Level!

Name: _____

Date: _____

Score: _____

Evaluate yourself based on your current performance, relative to new industry standards.	Level 1	Level 2	Level 3	Level 4	Level 5 Leader
	Unsatisfactory	Below Standard	Meets Standard	Above Standard	Outstanding Leader
1. Technical Skills	1	2	3	4	5
2. Presentation & Communication Skills	1	2	3	4	5
3. Self-Management & Organizational Skills	1	2	3	4	5
4. Attitude & Energy Level Skills	1	2	3	4	5
5. Powerful & Effective Team Building Skills	1	2	3	4	5
6. Overcoming Challenges to meet annual Goals	1	2	3	4	5
7. Initiative Skills	1	2	3	4	5
8. Leadership Skills	1	2	3	4	5
9. Integrity & Commitment Skills	1	2	3	4	5
10. Quality Professional Service Skills	1	2	3	4	5

Add up all your score for an **Overall Total** _____

Re-Focus On Your Higher Vision - A Tip from Jack Welch

"Rule 2 - Leaders make sure people not only see the vision, they live and breathe it.

It goes without saying that leaders have to set the team's vision and must do. But there's so much more to the "vision thing" than that. As a leader, you have to make the vision come alive.

How do you achieve that? First of all, do not speak in jargon. Goals cannot sound noble but vague. Targets cannot be so blurry they can't be hit. Your direction has to be so vivid that if you randomly woke one of your employees in the middle of the night and asked him, "Where are we going?" he could still answer in a half-asleep stupor, "We're going to keep improving our service to individual contracts and expand our market by aggressively reaching out to small wholesalers."

Vision is an essential element of the leader's job. But no vision is worth the paper it's printed on unless it is communicated constantly and reinforced with rewards. Only then will it leap off the page-and come to life."

**Winning by
Jack Welch with Suzy Welch**

What can we learn from Jack Welch's "Vision" concept?

When anyone asks you, or when you ask yourself, "Where are we going?" you must be able to effectively communicate your goals and objectives, 1-2-3-4. Maintaining our goals and objectives in the forefront of our minds will empower us to do 3 things:

1.   A clear vision allows us to **always focus our time, energy and thoughts on doing what must be done** in order to achieve our goals and objectives. At this level of empowerment, we are less likely to allow negative drama to block our success.

2.   A clear vision will give us direction and clarity. At this level of empowerment, we **make effective decisions** in our personal and professional lives that support our goals and objectives.

3.   When faced with a challenge, a clear vision gives our minds information to process in order to **discover solutions.** At this level of empowerment, we do not allow negative life challenges to block the successful accomplishment of our goals and objectives.

Ramifications of NOT having a Clear Vision:

If you don't know where you are going, how will you ever get there? When we do not have a clear vision that communicates our goals and objectives, we become frustrated, overwhelmed and discouraged. In addition, it dis-empowers us to the point that:

1.   We allow negative drama to consume our time, energy and thoughts; at that point, we become scattered and unfocused.

2.   We have no direction or clarity, so we make decisions that do not support our goals and objectives.

3.   We allow for negative challenges to block us from accomplishing our goals and objectives. At this point, we

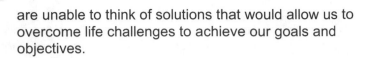
are unable to think of solutions that would allow us to overcome life challenges to achieve our goals and objectives.

Conclusion in a Nutshell:
If it is our intent to succeed in the accomplishment of our goals and desires, then we must have a clear vision in the forefront of our minds. This will allow us to overcome life challenges in order to materialize our goals and objectives.

Assignment for Growth and Development:
Take the time to sit down and think about what you desire to materialize in your life. Next, write down these goals and objectives on paper. Lastly, internalize these goals and objectives by placing a copy on your mirror, so that you can review them several times a day. This assignment will prepare you for the next time someone asks you or if you ask yourself, "Where are we going?" you can, without thinking about it, communicate, "I am going to achieve A-B-C-D and this is how I am going to achieve it".

What Do You Think? Notes, Comments, Commitments:

_____

_____

_____

_____

_____

_____

_____

_____

Know Yourself

A Tip for Developing Good Presentation & Communication Skills

"Know The Answers To the Following Questions Before Any Interview or Presentation"

To Present Powerfully Is A Self-Discover Process

1. **Who are you?**
    I am powerful, intelligent, courageous, unique and beautiful. (How does this get played out in your daily life?)

2. **What is your purpose in this world?**
    My purpose is to be a great person and to share that greatness with this world. (How do you go about sharing your greatness with this world?)

4. **What are you personal and professional goals and desires?**
    I desire to:
    a. Develop a stronger Mind, Body and Spirit
    b. Develop Loving Relationships with all people
    c. Advance Professionally and
    d. Increase my financial net worth

4. **How do you overcome your life challenges?**
    I effectively overcome my life challenges in a powerful manner. (Give an example.)

5. **How should you present and communicate yourself in the world?**
    I Present and Communicate myself to the world in a Loving and Powerful manner.

My 10 Top Priorities
For Professional Advancement

Project	Project Description	Status	Completion Date
1.			
2.			
3.			
4.			
5.			
6.			
7.			
8.			
9.			
10.			

I Am Powerful Enough

Where do I start? "By Taking Action Now"

I would like to introduce the 5 Leadership Principles in the form of Positive Rituals. I like what The Power of Full Engagement had to say about positive rituals.

Positive Rituals - A Tip from The Power of Full Engagement

"Positive energy rituals are powerful on three levels. They help us to ensure that we effectively manage energy in the service of whatever mission we are on. They reduce the need to rely on our limited conscious will and discipline to take action. Finally, rituals are a powerful means by which to translate our values and priorities into action – to embody what matters most to us in our everyday behaviors."

The Power of Full Engagement,
Managing Energy, not Time Is the Key to High
Performance and Personal Renewal
Jim Loer and Tony Schwartz

In light of the simple but powerful concept, I thought it would be great if each of us could make the 5 Leadership Principles a Positive Ritual. Affirm these 5 Leadership Principles and see if it empowers you.

Affirm 5 Leadership Principles for The Successful Leader

1. **LEAD - I am responsible for the achievement of the goals and objectives of my company.**

2. **LEAD - I present and communicate myself powerfully with integrity.**

3. **LEAD – My top priority is to empower team members to operate at their fullest potential.**

4. **LEAD - I Have the Emotional Fortitude – to be "listenable" and to effectively confront negative people and situations directly, and accept full responsibility for the outcome.**

5. **LEAD - In the face of challenges, I retain faith that my team and I will prevail in the end, not weakened but stronger.**

Leadership Principle #1 Affirm

LEAD - I am responsible for providing great service and achieving the goals and objectives of my company.

The Successful Leader takes personal responsibility for providing great service and the achievement of the goals and objectives of their Company, no excuses.

Personal Responsibility - A Tip From Oprah Winfrey!

  TakeResponsibility For Your Success

In May 2002 *Fortune Magazine* ran an article on Oprah Winfrey when she became a Billionaire. In the article, Oprah equated her personal and professional success with TAKING PERSONAL RESPONSIBLITY. TAKE RESPONSIBILITY FOR THE GOOD AND TAKE RESPONSIBILITY FOR THE BAD.

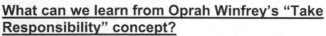
What can we learn from Oprah Winfrey's "Take Responsibility" concept?

When we take personal responsibility for giving great service and the achievement of our goals and desires, we can achieve 3 things.

When we take personal responsibility:

1. We open the door to **possibility thinking**. This concept will allow us to focus on solutions rather then complaining about challenges. At this level of possibility thinking, we are empowered to discover solutions to whatever challenge we face to achieve our goals and objectives.

2. We **embrace the power within** to overcome our daily challenges that could block our success. This will allow us to overcome our own internal fears, doubts and insecurities that may dis-empower us from accomplishing our daily objectives. Moreover, it empowers us to use our challenges as an opportunity to grow to our next level of success.

3. We stop blaming and **re-focus our time, energy and thoughts on being productive and providing great service.** When faced with negativity and when we start to feel defeated, this concept will empower us to always, always, always re-focus ourselves on the positive versus the negative. At this level of focused thinking, we are empowered to change the things that we have power and control over and leave the rest up to the universe to deal with.

Ramifications For Not Taking Responsibility:

When we do not strive to take personal responsibility for giving great service and accomplishing our goals and objectives, it can dis-empower us to the point that:

1. We are not open to possibility thinking and we continue to focus on the negative.

2. We continue to allow our fears, doubts and insecurities to block us from providing good services and acting to achieve our goals.

3. We continue to blame negative people, situations and circumstances for why we have not accomplished what we say is important to us.

Conclusion In A Nutshell:
When we strive to take personal responsibility, even when we don't want to, we empower ourselves to operate at our highest potential. At this level of empowerment, we become stronger, more powerful people who are able to overcome life challenges to give great service and achieve our personal and professional goals and objectives.

Also, Note!
We may not be responsible for the life challenges that come to us, but we are responsible for our reactions and responses to those challenges. If our intent is to succeed in life, then we must take personal responsibility for overcoming every life challenge in a powerful manner. Again, this will empower us to become more solution-oriented versus blame-oriented.

Assignment for Growth & Development:
The next time you observe yourself blaming your lack of success or unhappiness on negative people, situations and circumstances, affirm the following to yourself.

I take back the power! I take back the power. I take back the power. I now take the Lead. I am powerful enough to accept full responsibility for giving great service and achieving my goals and desires.

Next, re-focus your time, energy and thoughts on being powerful and productive. Focus yourself on taking one action step to move yourself closer to your goals. Remember, it does not

matter if this action step is big or small, because ultimately your goal is to empower yourself to become a more powerful person. Over time, you will develop an inner strength to overcome any life challenge to achieve your goals and desires.

What Do You Think? Notes, Comments, Commitments:

_____

_____

_____

_____

_____

_____

_____

What Do You Think? Notes, Comments, Commitments:

_____

_____

_____

_____

_____

_____

_____

Affirm Leadership Principle #2

LEAD - I present and communicate myself powerfully with integrity.

The Successful Leader always presents and communicates himself or herself powerfully with integrity.

Authenticity - A Tip from Execution By Larry Bossidy

"Authenticity: A psychological term, authenticity means pretty much what you might guess; you are real, not a fake. Your outer person is the same as your inner person, not a mask that you put on. Who you are is the same as what you do and say. Only authenticity builds trust, because sooner or later people spot the fakers. Whatever leadership ethics you may preach, people will watch what you do."

Execution
The Discipline of Getting Things Done
Larry Bossidy, Chairman, Honeywell International
Ram Charan, Author of *What the CEO Wants You To Know*

What can we learn from Execution's "Be Authentic" concept?
Being authentic is a great way to influence people to Execute without a lot of negative drama. Presenting and communicating ourselves powerfully, with integrity, will empower us to be 3 things: Authentic, Honest and Patient.

1. **Be Authentic** - Being authentic allows us to **discover who we are and keep growing.** When we know who we are, we are comfortable with our strengths and are not destroyed by our shortcomings.

2. **Be Honest** – Being honest allows us to confront the reality of our strengths and weaknesses, so that we can **build on our strengths and correct our weaknesses**. In addition, being honest will empower us to present and communicate ourselves to people, not as superior or inferior, but equal unto everyone.

3. **Be Patient** – Being patient will allow us to save ourselves a ton of time, energy and thought. This will free us up to **refocus our time, energy and thoughts on being powerful and productive**, with a good attitude.

Ramifications of not presenting and communicating ourselves Powerfully with Integrity:

When we do not strive to present and communicate ourselves powerfully with integrity, we dis-empower ourselves to the point that:

1. We develop a false sense of self. When we have a false sense of self, we don't know who we are and we allow our insecurities and shortcomings to destroy our potential.

2. We lie to ourselves and other people about our strengths and weaknesses. Moreover, we continue to stay in denial about the internal changes we know we need to make in order to present and communicate more effectively.

3. We are impatient with people and ourselves. Furthermore, we have a bad attitude and a negative disposition.

Conclusion In A Nutshell:
Striving to present and communicate ourselves powerfully, with integrity, even when we do not feel like it, will empower us to operate at our highest potential to provide great service and achieve our goals and objectives. In addition, it allows us to influence the people around us to "do better than their best" in whatever they decide to do.

Assignment for Growth & Development:
The next time you observe yourself NOT being effective in influencing people, check your presentation and communication skills. You can do this by asking yourself the following 3 questions:

1. Am I Being Authentic?
2. Am I Being Honest?
3. Am I Being Patient?

Answering these 3 questions should give you some insight as to what you need to improve in order to influence people in a positive manner.

What Do You Think? Notes, Comments, Commitments:

_____
_____
_____
_____
_____
_____

Affirm Leadership Principle #3

LEAD – My top priority is to empower team members to operate at their fullest potential.

The Successful Leader's top priority is to empower themselves and team members to operate at their fullest potential.

Team Building - A Tip From Kristy, a Cheerleader

In 2005, while Kristy and her squad were cheering their team to victory, Kristy fell from 18 feet. She suffered a concussion, burst lung and fractured 2 vertebrae in her back. While still in recovery, Kristy appeared on the Ellen Show. During the interview, Ellen asked her was she upset with her team members for letting her fall. Kristy responded by saying, "No. We are all a squad. Anything that goes right or wrong is a group accomplishment." Ellen then asked her why she did the fight song while they carried her off the floor. Kristy replied, "I am a cheerleader and I am still a part of the team and I did not want my team to get distracted from winning the game."

Kristy gave us a Real-Time Visual of what it means to be a powerful team player.

Moreover, she gave us a Real-Time Visual of what it means to regain your power after a devastating fall. The Successful Leader regains their power after a devastating fall because they have a strong character, energy and spirit about them.

What can we learn from Kristy's "Empower Team Members" concept?

We can learn that when we are working to accomplish a goal, sometimes the team will fall. Even though it may hurt, we are still required to be powerful people if our deepest intent is to Succeed in life. This will empower us to come back from difficulty not weakened, but stronger.

When a team member is faltering and is not stepping up to the plate, be patient with them. An effective Leader uses this as an opportunity to encourage and empower rather than criticize, blame or dis-empower the team member.

Empowering Team Members will allow us to do 3 things:

1. Empowering Team Members allows us to **overcome relationship challenges** to give great service and still accomplish team goals and objectives.

2. Empowering Team Members allows us to **eliminate the negative drama** that could drain energy and distract the team from giving great service and accomplishing its goals and objectives.

3. Empowering Team Members **gives us an opportunity to realize our goals and desires** and allows our team members to do the same.

Ramifications of not Empowering Team Members:

When we do not strive to empower team members to operate at their highest potential, we dis-empower ourselves and the team to the point that:

1. We allow relationship challenges to block us from coming up with solutions to accomplish team goals and objectives.

2. We continue to get caught up in the negative drama that can distract the team from "doing what must be done to achieve team goals and objectives".

3. We lose the opportunity to provide great service and realize our potential to achieve team goals and desires.

Conclusion In A Nutshell:
If it is our intent to succeed in life, more than likely, we will need a strong powerful team to assist us in making our dreams come true. In light of this concept, we must seek to develop harmonious, successful relationships with all people in our personal and professional lives. The ability to get along harmoniously with people and our environment will give us the freedom to create greatness in this lifetime.

Assignment for Growth & Development:
The next time you observe yourself feeling frustrated or resentful towards a team member in your personal or profession life, remember the following:

When a team member is not operating at their potential, effective Leaders use this as an opportunity to encourage and empower rather than criticize and dis-empower the team member.

You may encourage and empower the team member by communicating to them the following:

> *John Doe, I understand that you may have fears, so do I. However, if our intent is to move this organization to the next level, then we must confront and resolve our barriers in order to move forward.*

> *Allow me to suggest that we make an appointment to discuss some goals and objectives for how I can assist us in overcoming our barriers. OK!*

More than likely, this will empower your team member to relax and re-focus on operating at their highest potential to overcome their fears, doubts and insecurities. At this level of empowerment, they are in a better position to effectively overcome their daily challenges to succeed more consistently.

What Do You Think? Notes, Comments, Commitments:

_____

_____

_____

_____

_____

_____

_____

What Do You Think? Notes, Comments, Commitments:

_____

_____

_____

_____

_____

_____

_____

Affirm Leadership Principle #4

LEAD - I Have the Emotional Fortitude – to be "listenable" and to effectively confront negative people and situations directly, and accept full responsibility for the outcome.

The Successful Leader has the Emotional Fortitude – to be "listenable" and to effectively confront negative people and situations, directly and accept full responsibility for the outcome.

Emotional Fortitude - A Tip From Execution by Larry Bossidy

"The Discipline of Getting Things Done"

"Everyone pays lip service to the idea that leading an organization requires strength of character. In execution, it's absolutely critical. Without what we call emotional fortitude, you can't be honest with yourself, deal honestly with business and organizational realities, or give people forthright assessments. You can't tolerate the diversity of viewpoints, mental architectures, and personal backgrounds that organizations need in their members in order to avoid becoming ingrown. If you can't do these things, you can't execute.

It takes emotional fortitude to be open to whatever information you need, whether it's what you like to hear or not. Emotional fortitude gives you the courage to accept points of view that are the opposite of yours and deal with conflict, and the confidence to encourage and accept challenges in group settings. It enables you to accept and deal with your own weaknesses, be firm with people who aren't performing, and to handle the ambiguity inherent in a fast-moving, complex organization.

Emotional fortitude comes from self-discovery and self-mastery. It is the foundation of people skills. Good leaders learn their specific personal strengths and weaknesses, especially in dealing with other people, then build on the strengths and correct the weaknesses. They earn their leadership when the followers see their inner strength, inner confidence, and ability to help team members deliver results, while at the same time expanding their own capabilities.

A solid, long-term leader has an ethical frame of reference that gives her the power and energy to carry out even the most difficult assignment. She never wavers from what she thinks is right. This characteristic is beyond honesty or beyond integrity, beyond treating people with dignity. It's a business leadership ethic."

Execution - The Discipline of Getting Things Done
Larry Bossidy, Chairman, Honeywell International
Ram Charan, Author of What The CEO Wants You To Know

What can we extract from Executions' "Emotional Fortitude" concept:
If it is our intent to succeed in life, then we must develop the emotional fortitude (power within) to do what must be done in order to effectively Execute goals and objectives. Developing emotional fortitude will empower us to…

1. Control our negative emotions, such as: fear, doubt and insecurity.

2. Be honest with ourselves about the *internal changes* we know we need to make in order to achieve goals and desires.

3. Stop allowing negative people to manipulate or control us into doing something that is not in our hearts to do.

4. Accept constructive criticism in love and work on the issue without excuses.

5. Effectively confront people directly when they are not performing at the level or when they have over-stepped their boundaries.

6. "Stand Down" when it is not appropriate to react or respond to a negative person or challenge.

7. Not allow people to inflict us with their negative energy, beliefs and opinions.

8. Say "NO" or "YES" to a person and follow through on our decision.

9. Admit when we are wrong and apologize when we have made an error.

10. Develop emotional fortitude that will empower us to make effective decisions in our personal and professional life, which will leads to the accomplishment of our goals and desires.

Being able to execute the above items will allow us to save a ton of time, energy and thought. At this level of empowerment, we can re-apply that time, energy and thought to giving great service and the accomplishment of annual goals and objectives.

Ramifications For Not Having Emotional Fortitude:
When we do not have the emotional fortitude to execute the above items, we dis-empower ourselves to the point that:

1. We allow our negative emotions to overpower us and drain our energy.

2. We cannot stand-up for our core values and beliefs.

3. We continue to allow negative people, situations and circumstances to control and manipulate us.

4. We cannot accept constructive criticism and address internal barriers.

5. We cannot tell people how we feel or what we think because we fear confrontation or rejection.

6. We cannot "stand down" when our intuition tells us, "it is not a good time to respond" because we can't control our negative emotions.

7. We allow unconscious people to inflict their negative perceptions and opinions onto us.

8. We cannot say "No" or "Yes" to people and follow through on our decisions.

9. We cannot admit or apologize when we "know" we are wrong.

10. We make decisions that do not support our goals and objectives.

Assignment for Growth & Development:
The next time you observe yourself not confronting people directly, procrastinating or making excuses for not meeting your daily quotas, Affirm to yourself the following:

<u>I Am Courageous</u> – I fear nothing or no one. I am the presence and the power of love. Love is the most powerful force on earth. Therefore, I am powerful enough to overcome my fears, doubts and insecurities to achieve my heart's desires. I can do all things with love, which supports and strengthens me.

Repeating this affirmation to yourself will empower you to overcome your fears, doubts and insecurities to do what must be done in order to effectively execute your daily objectives, give great service and achieve your goals and objectives.

What Do You Think? Notes, Comments, Commitments:

_____

_____

_____

_____

_____

Affirm Leadership Principle #5

LEAD - In the face of challenges, I retain faith that my team and I will prevail in the end, not weakened but stronger.

The Successful Leader, in the face of challenges, retains faith that the team will prevail in the end and emerge not weakened but stronger.

Retain Faith - A Tip from Good To Great by Jim Collins

**"Why some companies make the leap…
and others don't"**

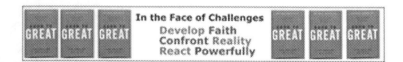

"The Stockdale Paradox (page 85) Life is unfair - sometimes to our advantage, sometimes to our disadvantage. We will all experience disappointments and crushing events somewhere along the way, setbacks for which there is no "reason," no one to blame. What separates people, Stockdale taught me, is not the presence or absence of difficulty, but how they deal with the inevitable difficulties of life. The Stockdale Paradox, "YOU must retain faith that you will prevail in the end and you must also confront the most brutal facts of your current reality", has proved powerful for coming back from difficulties not weakened, but stronger – not just for me, but for all those who've learned the lesson and tried to apply it.

Like much of what we found in our research, the key elements of greatness are deceptively simple and straightforward. The good-to-great leaders were able to strip away so much noise and clutter and just focus on the few things that would have the greatest

impact. They were able to do so in large part because they operated from both sides of the Stockdale Paradox, never letting one side overshadow the other. If you are able to adopt this dual pattern, you will dramatically increase the odds of making a series of good decisions and ultimately discovering a simple, yet deeply insightful concept for making the really big choices. And once you have that simple, unifying concept, you will be very close to making a sustained transition to breakthrough results."

Good To Great,
Why Some Companies Make the Leap… and Others Don't
A National Bestseller
By Jim Collins

What Do You Think? Notes, Comments, Commitments:

_____
_____
_____
_____

What Do You Think? Notes, Comments, Commitments:

_____
_____
_____
_____
_____

What can we learn from this "Good To Great" concept?

When we are confronted with life challenges, personally or professionally, it is crucial that we remember the Stockdale Paradox, "YOU must retain faith that you will prevail in the end and you must also confront the most brutal facts of your current reality".

Affirming this concept to ourselves will allow us to do 3 things: Develop Faith, Confront Reality and Respond Powerfully

1. **Develop Faith** – Developing faith allows us to develop our belief and confidence in our ability to succeed in the face of challenges. This will empower us to re-focus on possibility thinking. Which leads to powerful solutions and results.

2. **Confront Reality** – To confront reality simply means to see things as they are, not as we wish them to be, and to develop the power within, to do what must be done, not what is comfortable for us. This will empower us to accept the truth and deal with it effectively.

3. **React and Respond Powerfully** – Effective Leaders always react and respond to life challenges Powerfully, no matter what. To react and respond powerfully simply means to not allow for any life challenge to distract you from realizing your highest potential and possibility.

Ramifications of NOT having faith in the face of life challenges:

When we do not strive to have faith, in the face of life challenges, we dis-empower ourselves to the point that:

1. We do not have the self-confidence or belief in ourselves to succeed.

2. We continue to stay in denial or live in a fantasy world until we hit rock bottom or are defeated.

3. We react and respond to negative people and situations

with negativity, which drains our energy and distracts us from focusing on our goals.

4. We allow our life challenges to distract us from realizing our potential to create greatness in this lifetime.

Assignment for Growth and Development:
The next time you observe yourself feeling overwhelmed by negative life challenges, make it a practice to re-focus your time, energy and thoughts on being powerful and productive, regardless of how you feel. If you have trouble, repeat the following affirmation to yourself as often as you need to in order to do what must be done to succeed:

> **I Am Powerful** – I am spiritually, mentally and physically strong enough to overcome my life challenges to give great service and achieve my goals and desires. I am powerful enough to achieve the love, joy, peace and great riches I truly desire and deserve!

This will empower you to keep moving forward towards your goals and objectives, no matter what. Over time, you will become a stronger and more powerful person to overcome your challenges powerfully to succeed personally and professionally.

What Do You Think? Notes, Comments, Commitments:

_____
_____
_____
_____
_____
_____
_____
_____

Self-Management for Personal & Professional Advancement

Self-Management Affirmations

1. I Know My 4 Top Priorities

2. I Forgive, let it go, and move on

3. I Stand In the Consciousness Level Of Success

4. I Just Do It "Now"

5. I Don't Take "Negative Attacks" Personally and I Don't Get Emotional about them

6. I Observe The Signs, Listen to My Intuition & Plan Accordingly

7. I am not into Self-Promotion; I Let My Work Speak For Itself

8. I Clarify, Confirm & Always Follow-Up and Follow-Through

9. I Set The Example Of Success, Regardless of my position in life

10. I Let People Know Where I Stand by Affirming My Rules of Engagement

11. I Speak to People Directly and Let It Go

12. I Know When to Stand-Down and I Know When to Stand Up For Myself

13. I Have Stopped being a "People Pleaser"

14. I Believe people when they show me who they are

Self-Management Evaluation

Self-Management Concept #1

<u>**I Know My 4 Top Priorities**</u> – a.) I have a list of my 4 most important priorities and their status in writing and in the forefront of my mind. Or, b.) I have too much to do and not enough time to do it. Everything is a priority.

Self-Management Concept #2

<u>**I Forgive, let it go, and move on**</u> – a) I have forgiven myself and/or people for any wrongdoings and I am re-focusing that energy on the materialization of my deepest goals and desires. Or, b) I beat myself up because of past mistakes or setbacks. I still get hurt and disappointed when someone disrespects me; moreover, I don't stand up for myself. This drains my energy and takes me off focus.

Self-Management Concept #3

<u>**I Stand In the Consciousness Level Of Success**</u> – Focus On The Positive and Eliminate the Negative – a) I am thinking powerfully. "I can. I will. It is done. I feel great, etc." Or, b.) I find myself getting caught up in negative thinking. "I cannot do it. I am not good enough. I know I am going to fail. I do not feel well."

Self-Management Concept #4

<u>**I Just Do It "Now"**</u> – a.) I know what needs to be done and don't spend a lot of time and energy procrastinating, I just do it. Or, b) I spend a lot of time and energy worrying and thinking about tasks I already know how to do. I procrastinate on doing tasks I know need to be done.

Self-Management Concept #5

I Don't Take "Negative Attacks" Personally and I Don't Get Emotional About them! – a.) I react and respond to negative attacks in a powerful manner, regardless of the person or situation. Or b.) I find myself getting offended or feeling angry when someone says or does something that dis-empowers me. Negative attacks continue to drain my energy and take me off focus.

Self-Management Concept #6

I Observe The Signs, Listen to My Intuition & Plan Accordingly a.) I listen to my intuition and I make effective decisions that support the achievement of my goals and objectives. Or b.) I find myself saying, "I had a feeling that was going to happen. I should have followed my gut instinct," or, "I knew that they were going to rip me off/take advantage of me."

Self-Management Concept #7

I am not into Self-Promotion; I Let My Work Speak For Itself a.) I am speaking less and letting my great work speak for itself. Or, b.) I spend a lot of time and energy telling people what I am *going to do*. I spend a lot of time and energy trying to win people's approval by always talking about my past successes.

Self-Management Concept #8

I Clarify, Confirm & Always Follow-Up and Follow-Through a.) I am doing everything in my power to successfully complete projects and I am taking full advantage of the opportunities now being presented to me. Or, b.) I have projects that failed or opportunities that I have missed because of misperceptions and communication gaps. I find myself saying to people, after the fact, "I didn't understand what you wanted, I didn't know what you meant. I thought that *'they'* were going to take care of it."

Self-Management Concept #9

I Set The Example Of Success, Regardless of my position in life – a) I am doing less talking and more being the example of that which I desire people to "Get", Understand, or Internalize for the success of the whole. Or, b) I spend most of my time and energy trying to get people to do what they need to do to be successful, but at the same time, I am ignoring what I need to do in order to be successful.

Self-Management Concept #10

I Let People Know Where I Stand by Affirming My Rules of Engagement – a) I effectively communicate to all people my rules of engagement. In addition, when people overstep their boundaries I am powerful enough to stop them. Letting them know, "This is what I agreed to." Or b) I am not communicating myself effectively to people because they are constantly overstepping their boundaries. Moreover, I am not strong enough to stand up to them and tell them, "NO, this is not what I agreed to and I am not going to agree to something that I did not agreed to."

Self-Management Concept #11

I Speak to People Directly and Let It Go – a.) I effectively communicate my bottom line to all people without being long-winded or rambling.   Or, b) I find myself spending tons of time and energy trying to get people to understand an important concept or point that is crucial to results or success. (this could apply to family members or co-workers)

Self-Management Concept #12

I Know When to Stand-Down and I Know When to Stand Up For Myself – a.) When people or environments appear to be chaotic or out of control, I know when to stand down and I know when to stand up for myself. Or, b.) I find myself allowing negative situations or people to spin out of control, to the point that I feel negative and I am not heard, acknowledged or considered.

Self-Management Concept #13

I Have Stopped being a "People Pleaser" – a) I enjoy my life and do things to please my heart and soul. Or, b) I go to the extreme to please people hoping to be loved and accepted, only to get hurt and be disappointed in the end.

Self-Management Concept #14

"I Believe people when they show me who they are." – a) I believe people when they tell me who they are. Or, b) I ignore the warning signs and continue to allow people to manipulate and control me into doing things I do not desire to do. I try to convince myself, "maybe they'll change," when secretly I know that they will not change.

Self-Management for Personal Advancement

Self-Management Concept #1

I know My 4 Top Priorities – a.) I have a list of my 4 most important priorities and their status in writing and in the forefront of my mind. Or, b.) I have too much to do and not enough time to do it. Everything is a priority

If you answer "a", then BRAVO TO YOU and keep up the Great Work that you are doing in the world!

_____If you answer "b", please realize that if your deepest intent is to succeed in life, then you must keep your list of priorities and a status report in the forefront of your mind. In addition, these priorities must be in writing and posted where you can see them everyday. This will decrease your stress level and prevent you from feeling out of control with no direction. Each time you start to feel overwhelmed or frustrated, you must re-focus that time and energy on reviewing your 4 biggest priorities and their status. In addition, you must consistently do something on your priority list to move yourself forward. Getting your priorities straight will assist you in managing your time, energy and thoughts in order to accomplish your goals and objectives.

Self-Management Concept #2

I Forgive, let it go, and move on – a) I have forgiven myself and/or people for any wrongdoings and I am re-focusing that energy on the materialization of my deepest goals and desires. Or, b) I beat myself up because of past mistakes or setbacks. I still get hurt and disappointed when someone disrespects me; moreover, I don't stand up for myself. This drains my energy and takes me off focus.

If you answer "a", then BRAVO TO YOU and keep up the Great Work that you are doing in the world!

_____ If you answer "b" to the above statements, please realize that un-forgiveness is an energy drainer that will keep you from operating at your highest potential to succeed. Moreover, un-forgiveness will eventually make you physically sick. If it is your deepest intent to succeed, when you make a mistake or have a setback - immediately forgive yourself. When someone hurts or disrespects you, you must immediately forgive that person. To forgive, let go and move on simply means to learn the lesson, eliminate the negative conversation from your mind, and refocus that energy on materializing your heart's desires. Forgiving, letting it go, and moving on will give you the energy and confidence you need to overcome life challenges to succeed. Please note, if you have trouble forgiving, you may need to seek help from your higher power. This will allow you to tap into a higher power greater than yourself in order to forgive. This is an important key to Self-Management.

Self-Management Concept #3

I Stand In the Consciousness Level Of Success – Focus On The Positive and Eliminate the Negative – a) I am thinking powerfully. "I can. I will. It is done. I feel great, etc." Or, b.) I find myself getting caught up in negative thinking. "I cannot do it. I am not good enough. I know I am going to fail. I do not feel well."

If you answer "a", then BRAVO TO YOU and keep up the Great Work that you are doing in the world!

_____ If answer "b", then get in the habit of replacing those negative thoughts with positive thoughts. "I can. I will. It is done. I give thanks." Standing in the consciousness level of success simply means having a positive frame of mind. This allows you to focus on the positive versus the negative. Now, this does not mean to deny or ignore the negative. However, focusing on the positive versus the negative will empower you to develop the mindset and positive attitude required in order to believe in your ability to succeed. In addition, standing in the consciousness level of success will empower you to be become more goal and solution oriented. At this level of focused thinking and attention, you will do what must be done to materialize your goals and objectives.

Self-Management Concept #4

I Just Do It "Now" – a.) I know what needs to be done and don't spend a lot of time and energy procrastinating, I just do it. Or, b) I spend a lot of time and energy worrying and thinking about tasks I already know how to do. I procrastinate on doing tasks I know needs to be done.

If you answer "a", then BRAVO TO YOU and keep up the Great Work that you are doing in the world!

_____ If you answer "b" to the above statements, then get in the mindset of "don't procrastinate – just do it". Remember, spending a lot of time and energy thinking about tasks or thinking about things that have nothing to do with the project usually means that you are stalling or procrastinating. You already know that stalling and procrastinating does not work. So, the next time you observe yourself stalling or procrastinating on a task or find yourself thinking about things that have nothing to do with the project, I encourage you to affirm to yourself over and over, "Don't procrastinate – just do it". This will empower you to re-focus your time and energy on doing what must be done in order to materialize your goals and objectives.

Self-Management Concept #5

<u>**I Don't Take "Negative Attacks" Personally and I Don't Get Emotional About them!**</u> – a.) I react and respond to negative attacks in a powerful manner, regardless of the person or situation. Or, b.) I find myself getting offended or feeling angry when someone says or does something that dis-empowers me. Negative attacks continue to drain my energy and take me off focus.

If you answer "a", then BRAVO TO YOU and keep up the Great Work that you are doing in the world!

_____ If you answer "b" to the above statements, please realize that you cannot take people's attacks personally or get emotional about them. First, it is an energy drainer that will block you from focusing on your objectives. Second, in most cases, their attack on you has nothing to do with you and everything to do with their fears, doubts and insecurities. We all have insecurities, so be forgiving.

However, don't be naive. As you become more successful, more than likely, there will be negative attacks along the way that will attempt to block your success. These attacks can come in many forms, such as negative people, situations or circumstances. You must use these negative attacks as an opportunity to grow and develop. Don't worry; you have the power within you to overcome all negative attacks.

Not taking the attacks personally and not getting emotional about them will help you to conserve your energy and re-focus yourself on the accomplishment of your specific goals and desires. The goal in these negative situations is for you to exercise your inner power by focusing on your goals and doing what must be done to accomplish them. Applying this powerful concept will dramatically increase your motivation and energy level. It also will improve your people skills.

Self-Management Concept #6

I Observe The Signs, Listen to My Intuition & Plan Accordingly
a.) I listen to my intuition and I make effective decisions that support the achievement of my goals and objectives. Or, b.) I find myself saying, "I had a feeling that was going to happen. I should have followed my gut instinct," or, "I knew that they were going to rip me off/take advantage of me."

If you answer "a", then BRAVO TO YOU and keep up the Great Work that you are doing in the world!

_____ If you answer "b" to the above statements, learn to observe signs, listen to your intuition and plan accordingly. Remember, in most cases, before something devastating or unexpected occurs, there are always signs that led up to the occurrence. Generally, there are signs that lead up to the loss of a job, ending of a relationship or a need for change, etc. There are signs that led up to your being manipulated, controlled, or taken advantage of by someone. The consequences for not observing the signs, listening to your intuition and planning accordingly can be very damaging and sometimes catastrophic.

However, observing signs, listening to your intuition and planning accordingly will empower you to make effective decisions that support your ultimate goals and objectives. Moreover, it will prevent you from having to deal with unnecessary setbacks. Also note, never allow someone else's voice to overpower your inner voice.

Self-Management Concept #7

I am not into Self-Promotion; I Let My Work Speak For Itself

a.) I am speaking less and letting my great work speak for itself. Or, b.) I spend a lot of time and energy telling people what I am *going to do.* I spend a lot of time and energy trying to win people's approval by always talking about my past successes.

If you answer "a", then BRAVO TO YOU and keep up the Great Work that you are doing in the world!

_____ If you answer "b", please realize that this is a waste of time and energy and people usually don't appreciate it. If you're good, you don't have to talk about it because people will see it in your work. The time you spend with self-promotions must be re-focused on clarifying your vision, coming up with solutions for challenges and exploring new opportunities for growth and development. The more you focus on doing great work, the less you have to self-promote because the work will speak for itself.

What Do You Think? Notes, Comments, Commitments:

_____

_____

_____

_____

_____

_____

_____

_____

Self-Management For Professional Advancement

Self-Management Concept #8

I Clarify, Confirm & Always Follow-Up and Follow-Through

a.) I am doing everything in my power to successfully complete projects and I am taking full advantage of the opportunities now being presented to me. Or, b.) I have projects that failed or opportunities that I have missed because of misperceptions and communication gaps. I find myself saying to people, after the fact, "I didn't understand what you wanted, I didn't know what you meant. I thought that *'they'* were going to take care of it."

If you answer "a", then BRAVO TO YOU and keep up the Great Work that you are doing in the world!

_____ If you answer "b" to the above statements, then get into the habit of Clarifying and Confirming with people and Always Follow-up and Follow-through. Clarifying, confirming, following-up and following through simply means doing everything in your power to successfully take care of your responsibilities and not allowing for mis-communication gaps to block your success. Practicing this concept will allow you to take full advantage of great opportunities and successfully complete projects on time. In addition, it will allow you to develop good work habits and it will give you peace of mind.

Self-Management Concept #9

I Set The Example Of Success, Regardless of my position in life

– a) I am doing less talking and more being the example of that which I desire people to "Get", Understand, or Internalize for the success of the whole. Or, b) I spend most of my time and energy trying to get people to do what they need to do to be successful, but at the same time, I am ignoring what I need to do in order to be successful.

If you answer "a", then BRAVO TO YOU and keep up the Great Work that you are doing in the world!

_____ If your answer is "b" to the above statement, then make a commitment to yourself to be an example of success regardless of your position in life. Today, make a commitment to be more loving, professional, fair, competent and pleasant, regardless of your position in life. Setting the example of success will empower you to succeed consistently. Succeeding consistently will immediately produce significant results in the accomplishments of your goals. In addition, it will allow you to motivate and inspire the people around you that you desire to influence. Setting the example of success, regardless of your position in life, will increase your energy level, critical thinking skills and your self-confidence. Also, it will allow you to develop good work habits that support your personal and professional advancement.

Self-Management Concept #10

I Let People Know Where I Stand by Affirming My Rules of Engagement – a) I effectively communicate to all people my rules of engagement. In addition, when people overstep their boundaries I am powerful enough to stop them. Letting them know, "This is what I agreed to.", or b) I am not communicating myself effectively to people because they are constantly overstepping their boundaries. Moreover, I am not strong enough to stand up to them and tell them, "NO, this is not what I agreed to and I am not going to agree to something that I did not agree to."

If you answer "a", then BRAVO TO YOU and keep up the Great Work that you are doing in the world!

_____ If you answer "b" to the above statements, don't feel weak or powerless. Lean how to let people know where you stand by affirming your rules of engagement. Letting people know where you stand by affirming your rules of engagement simply means to let people know, directly, what you will or will not tolerate. This will allow you to regain your power, energy and confidence.

Remember, each time you allow people to overstep their boundaries, you lose power, energy and confidence.

For example, think of a person who oversteps their boundaries with you every chance they get. Now, you must let them know, directly or indirectly, where you stand by affirming your new rules of engagement: Communicate "Mary-Sue, when I start to feel disempowered, I am leaving this conversation. Tom, if you start to demean, belittle or attack me, without just cause, I will leave this conversation. Paula, if you start to talk negatively about other people or have nothing positive to say, I will leave this conversation. Maggie, if you start to curse at me, I will leave this communication."

When people start to overstep their boundaries, you will automatically enforce your rules of engagement. "Excuse me, Maggie, perhaps we can communicate later, when you feel better." Leave the conversation, without explanation, and do not feel bad or guilty. They will get over it and learn to respect you. Once you leave the conversation, you must refocus your time, energy and thoughts on the accomplishment of your daily objectives.

Self-Management Concept #11

I Speak to People Directly and Let It Go – a.) I effectively communicate my bottom line to all people without being long-winded or rambling. Or, b) I find myself spending tons of time and energy trying to get people to understand an important concept or point that is crucial to results or success. (this could apply to a family members or co-workers)

If you answer "a", then BRAVO TO YOU and keep up the Great Work that you are doing in the world!

_____ If you answer "b", then learn to speak to people directly and don't worry about whether they "got it", let it go and make sure that you "got it". Speaking to people directly and letting it go simply means to effectively communicate your bottom-line and make you point in 2 minutes or less and then move-on. Remember, belaboring a point is a waste of time and energy and can cause more damage than good. Why? If a person is not ready to "get it"– it does not matter what you say or how you say it, they are not going to "get it" until they are ready. You must respect where they are and not allow them to keep you from moving forward on your goals.

When you observe yourself spending a lot of time and energy trying to get people to understand an important concept or point that is crucial to results or success, speak to them directly, let it go and make sure that you "got it". Applying this concept will save you a ton of time and energy when communicating with unconscious people or people who are not sure of the direction they desire to move in their lives.

Self-Management Concept #12

<u>**I Know When to Stand-Down and I Know When to Stand-Up For Myself**</u> – a.) When people or environments appear to be chaotic or out of control, I know when to stand-down and I know when to stand-up for myself. Or, b.) I find myself allowing negative situations or people to spin out of control, to the point that I feeling negative and I am not heard, acknowledged or considered.

If you answer "a", then BRAVO TO YOU and keep up the Great Work that you are doing in the world!

_____ If you answer "b", when people appear to be out of control, then you must learn how to stand-down. Knowing when to stand-down simply means knowing when to stand-up and knowing when to sit-down and shut-up. Please note, this technique requires you to be sensitive to people and the environment. When people or the environment is chaotic or out of control, this should be a red flag for you to "stand-down". Why? Because more than likely, you will not be heard and you could do more damage than good.

Knowing when to stand-down can prevent negative situations from spinning out of control. In addition, it can save you from saying the right thing at the wrong time. Knowing when to stand-down or stand-up for what you believe will make you a stronger person and a more effective communicator.

Self-Management Concept #13

I Have Stopped being a "People Pleaser" – a) I enjoy my life and do things to please my heart and soul. Or, b) I go to the extreme to please people hoping to be loved and accepted, only to get hurt and be disappointed in the end.

If you answer "a", then BRAVO TO YOU and keep up the Great Work that you are doing in the world!

_____ If you answer "b", please realize that you cannot please people 100% percent of the time – the more they get, the more they want. The more money you give them, the more money they need. They never learn to create money for themselves. The more sympathy you give people, the more drama they create to obtain sympathy. The more energy you give them, the more they will take, and before long you have lost yourself. You must do things to please your heart and soul. If it pleases others, great, but if it doesn't, you will have to be at peace with this. When you are living your life based in growth and development and love and truth, all things will happen for the higher good of all.

Self-Management Concept #14

"I Believe people when they show me who they are."
a) I believe people when they tell me who they are and I act accordingly. Or, b) I continue to allow people to manipulate and control me into doing things I do not desire to do. I try to convince myself, "maybe they'll change," when secretly I know that they will

not change.

If you answer "a", then BRAVO TO YOU and keep up the Great Work that you are doing in the world!

_____ If you answered "b", always remember, your intuition is always speaking to you. Listen when people tell you, "I am in your life to destroy you by stealing your energy and holding you back," or conversely, "I am in your life to support you in love and assist you in growing and moving forward." Do not waste your time and energy on people who are not interested in growing and moving forward. This concept will save you a lot of time and energy when communicating with people.

Self-Management Concept #15

Create A Self-Management Concept for Yourself:

_____

_____

_____

_____

_____

_____

_____

Who Really Wants To Achieve Greatness?
How To Attract and Maintain Loyal Friends & Customers For Life

Give Great Service Personally & Professionally

Be Inspired:

Oprah Winfrey said, "One of my favorite quotes in life comes from Dr. Martin Luther King. He said, 'Everyone has the power for greatness, not for fame but greatness, because greatness is determined by service.' Dr. King began as an ordinary man, yet he accomplished more than many presidents. His life story stands as a testament of one man's ability to change the world with love and compassion. Let us always remember."

A Check List For Giving Great Service:

1. Service Self First "The Energy To Give Great Service"
2. Master Your Communication With Your Clients
3. Be Sincerely Interested In Meeting Your Clients' Needs
4. Know Your Product and/or Service and Communicate it Powerfully and Effectively
5. Never, Ever Argue or Be Impatient with a Client

5 Powerful Tips for Giving Great Service

Great Service Tip #1

Service Self First "The Energy To Give Great Service, personally and professionally" – To Service Self First simply means to take care of yourself before you communicate with a client or the world. Each day you must nurture, develop and renew your mind, body and spirit. Each day you must Meditate, Affirm, and Visualize who you desire to be and what you desire to achieve. This will give you energy, insight and a better understanding of how to effectively service your clients. Moreover, you will not be stressed or get burned-out. Remember, people like people who take care of themselves and they remain loyal to the people who give them great service. In addition, word of mouth is still the best advertisement. Service Self First!

What Do You Think? Notes, Comments, Commitments:

_____

_____

_____

_____

_____

_____

_____

_____

Great Service Tip #2

Master Your Communications With Your Clients –

Mastering your communications with clients will make you mindful of the following: Be on time. Say, "Hello, how are you?" Smile and have a positive attitude. Be professional and energized. Call your client by name if possible. If not, Sir or Ma'am is fine. Know your agenda for the client. Do not waste clients' time. Allow your clients to communicate their needs, concerns and desires. Listen, Listen, Listen to what your client is saying. This is important. Be humble, personable and patient with your clients. Effectively communicate yourself and your product or service to your client. Give great service and give your clients more than they expected. Holding yourself to a high standard of service will allow you to fulfill your purpose and materialize your ultimate personal and professional goals and desires.

What Do You Think? Notes, Comments, Commitments:

_____

_____

_____

_____

_____

_____

_____

Great Service Tip #3

Be Sincerely Interested In Meeting Your Clients' Needs –
Being sincerely interested in your clients' needs will allow you to
communicate with clients on a deeper level that benefits you and
them. This is important because it will help you to better meet their
needs. Remember, people know when they are being rushed,
bullied, or short-changed and they do not like it. If it is your
deepest intent to advance personally, professionally and
financially, you must seek to sincerely be interested in meeting the
needs, concerns and desires of your clients. Make them feel like
they are very important. Applying this concept will give you
positive energy. It is a great feeling when you know that you
sincerely have helped people in a positive way. Remember, the
more positive energy you put out into the world, the more
prosperity you will achieve. Be Sincerely Interested In Meeting
Your Clients' Needs!

What Do You Think? Notes, Comments, Commitments:

_____

_____

_____

_____

_____

_____

_____

_____

Great Service Tip #4

**Know Your Product and/or Service and Communicate it
Powerfully and Effectively** – This will tell your customer the
following:

- ➤ It lets them know that they made the right choice in doing
  business with you. This will allow them to relax a little.
  Remember, this is an important ingredient in effective
  communications.

- ➤ It lets them know that you are knowledgeable about all
  aspects of your products or services. This makes them feel
  even more comfortable. At this level, they are more likely
  to listen intensely to your ideas and concepts. This is an
  important ingredient for their decision-making process to
  buy and or continue doing business with you, or not.

- ➤ It lets the client know that they can trust and depend on you
  to solve their challenges or at least come up with other
  solutions. They feel like they are in good hands and they
  will get the best results for their hard earned money. This is
  crucial for building your reputation, repeat business and
  referrals.

- ➤ It lets the client know that they can count on you to step-up-
  to-the-plate and deliver great service, no matter what.

What Do You Think? Notes, Comments, Commitments:

_____

_____

_____

_____

_____

_____

Great Service Tip #5

Never, Ever Argue or Be Impatient with a Client – Granted, some negative clients may not deserve your "best". However, do not cut off your nose to spite your face; give every client high quality service. You must never fight negativity with negativity because it will only bring more negativity. Moreover, it will only dis-empower you from giving great service to your next customer. You would do better by crossing negative customers off your client list. Make a decision to not do repeat business with negative clients.

This may be difficult, but remember: First, you always have other options; so don't be consumed by negative clients. Second, when you give great service, you have no need to worry because the window of opportunity is always open to you and your possibilities are endless. Finally, before you write off a negative client, make sure that you did not give them a good reason to be negative. Never, Ever Argue or Be Impatient with a Client!

Give Great Service wherever you are in your personal and professional life. It will empower you to achieve the great life you ultimately desire and deserve.

What Do You Think? Notes, Comments, Commitments:

_____

_____

_____

_____

_____

_____

_____

_____

10 Tips For Professional Advancement

As the workplace becomes more competitive, diverse and global, interpersonal skills and professionalism are major keys to the success of any great team or work environment. This component is designed to remind us of proper etiquette/professionalism in the workplace. This will allow us to have a brief open discussion on how we should react and respond in a professional environment for success now. We will focus on addressing issues that tend to drain energy, create resentment and takes the team off focus. Issues to be addressed: Respect, Diversity, Tolerance and more.

10 Powerful Affirmations for Professional Advancement

1. I Treat All People with Love and Respect.

2. I take personal responsibility for my success and failures.

3. I handle all challenges in a powerful manner.

4. I only participate in conversations that are empowering.

5. I treat all people fairly and equally.

6. I accept constructive criticism and strive to be better and better!

7. I am a "take charge" person and take responsibility for completing my workload.

8. I am genuinely happy when other people are promoted or succeed – even when I am not.

9. I always give more than expected.

10. I only speak the highest truth that I know.

___**1. I Treat All People with Love and Respect!** Powerful professionals treat all people with love and respect regardless of position, situations or circumstances. It is unprofessional to abuse any person with your words, thoughts or behaviors. This can come in the form of a supervisor treating employees as inferior or an employee overstepping their boundaries with a co-worker. Treat all people with love and respect.

___**2. I take personal responsibility for my success and failures!** - Powerful Professionals always take personal responsibility for their mistakes. This empowers them to be better the next time. It is unprofessional to not take responsibility for your mistakes and then blame other people. For example, a major project was not completed on time and when asked by a supervisor what happened, the person blames everyone but themselves for the reason the project was not completed on time. Always take personal responsibility; you will earn more respect as a result.

Do you think that the supervisor knows when a person is making excuses and not taking responsibility?

How do you think a supervisor perceives a person who blames others for their mistakes?

___ **3. I handle all challenges in a powerful manner!** Remember, fighting negativity with negativity never works out in the end for anyone. Powerful professionals always keep in mind that there is always a positive way to handle negative people or situations. Bad behavior is unprofessional, whether in a meeting, dealing with a co-worker, or in any public form. This concept can come in the form of someone insulting you and you feeling justified to insult him or her in return. Do not allow unconscious people to pull you into their negative disposition. Handle all negative challenges in a powerful manner. You will earn the greatest respect from your co-worker as a result.

___**4. I only participate in conversations that are empowering.** If it is your intent to advance professionally then stick to conversations that empower and enlighten the professional environment. It is unprofessional to gossip or talk negatively about other people. Not only does gossiping and talking negative about other people drain energy and take people off focus, it is mean. Only have empowering conversations; this will motivate and empower you and the work environment.

___**5. I treat all people fairly and equally**. If it is your intent to be an effective leader, then you must treat all people equally. Playing favorites is unprofessional and can also cause friction among co-workers. What you do for one, you must get in the habit of doing for all, whether you like the person or not. You will gain major respect when you treat people fairly and equally.

___**6. I accept constructive criticism and strive to be better and better!** Powerful professionals know how to take constructive criticism seriously and strive to be better employees as a result. It is unprofessional to be in denial about your job performance. It can destroy you and the company. This can come in the form of someone telling you directly "you need to step-up in your performance" and you respond, "No I do not, because I do more than anyone on this job." Never ignore or make excuses for your shortcomings. Always accept constructive criticism and strive to be and do better and better. This mindset will empower you to be a stronger more marketable person as a result.

___ **7. I am a "take charge" person and take responsibility for completing my workload!** Powerful professionals take charge and accept full responsibilities for doing their own workload. It is unprofessional to get other people to do your work for you. This can come in the form of you just being too lazy to do it yourself or you feeling that the work is beneath you. You might say, "Well, they don't mind". In most cases they do mind but just do not have the courage to tell you directly, "Do Your Own Work". Be a "take charge" person and take responsibility for completing your own workload.

___ **8. I am genuinely happy when other people are promoted or succeed – even when I am not**. Powerful professionals understand 2 things, 1) if they can't be happy for others people's successes, then people will not be happy for their success, which makes their success or promotion bittersweet, and 2) If it is possible for other people to be promoted and succeed, then it means that it is possible for them to be promoted and succeed. Always be genuinely happy when other people are promoted or succeed.

___ **9. I always give more than expected.** Powerful professionals understand that in some cases, in order for the team to succeed, they will be required to do more than expected. It is unprofessional when the team needs you to do additional duties and you tell them "No". Or you tell the team, "Sure, I will do it, if you give me more money."

___ **10. I only speak the highest truth that I know.**
Powerful professionals know it is better to tell the truth than get caught-up in a web of lies! It is unprofessional to lie or not tell the truth. Regardless of the consequences, we must always speak the truth, even if it costs you a friend or two.

What Do You Think? Notes, Comments, Commitments:

_____

_____

_____

_____

_____

_____

_____

_____

What Do You Think? Notes, Comments, Commitments:

_____

_____

_____

_____

_____

_____

_____

_____

Team Building

(Overcome 20 Team Building/Relationship Challenges)

1. Do you know the goals and objectives of the team?
2. How would you effectively deal with a team member who is not motivated?
3. What would you do if a team member did not take responsibility for their mistake; moreover, they blamed you for the failure of the project?
4. What do you do when team members are gossiping and trying to enlist you in their drama?
5. How do you handle it when someone in the group is clearly getting special privileges from the leader?
6. What would you do if the leader of the team were about to make a terrible mistake; moreover, this leader is not interested in hearing your solution?
7. How do you effectively communicate to someone that they are wrong, without making them feel wrong or stupid?
8. How do you confront someone who has overstepped your boundary?
9. What should you do when you are not going to meet a deadline for a project?

10. What should you do if someone asks you to do something unethical?
11. What would you do if someone accused you of slander?
12. What should you do if a team member is late giving you documents or information needed to complete your end of the project?
13. What should you do when a team member becomes your enemy? How should you protect yourself?
14. How should you deal with a team member who acts superior and treats you as if you are inferior?
15. What should you do if you fear telling a team member the truth?
16. What should you do when someone loses patience with you?
17. How do you get people to do what you desire, without intimidating or manipulating them?
18. What is the responsibility of a team leader?
19. What should you do when you have made a mistake with a team member?
20. What should you do when the team does not share the same commitment and goals for excellence as you?

What Do You Think? Notes, Comments, Commitments:

_____

_____

_____

_____

_____

_____

_____

20 Tips To Overcoming Relationship Challenges

1. Do you know the goals and objectives of the team?
  a. If you don't know your team's goals and objectives, learn them and be able to effectively communicate them at all times.

  b. Understand your role in accomplishing the goals and objectives of the team.

2. How would you effectively deal with a team member who is not motivated?
  a. Increase your motivation and be patient with them.

  b. When they are being negative, focus your conversation on positive solutions.

  c. Re-affirm their power by saying to them, "I believe you are powerful enough to overcome the challenge."

  d. Do not allow them to steal your energy or waste your time.

3. What would you do if a team member did not take responsibility for their mistake; moreover, they blamed you for the failure of the project?

  a. Take responsibility for your nickel in the dime.

  b. If there is a miscommunication, then you must assume that you did not make yourself clear. This attitude will help you to prevent communication mistakes in the future.

  c. If a person misses a deadline, get in the habit of sending them a reminder in writing. This way, you will not be blamed if the project is not completed on time.

4. What do you do when team members are gossiping and trying to enlist you in their drama? Did you hear about…? What do you think about…? Aren't you just appalled by…?

    a. Be consciously aware that gossip is an energy drainer.

    b. As soon as the gossip queen starts to gossip, stop them.

    c. Tell them, "I am not interested in talking about anything that is not going to move us forward."

    d. If they persist, excuse yourself from their presence.

    e. If they still persist, let them know that they are overstepping your boundaries.

5. How do you handle it when someone in the group is clearly getting special privileges from the leader?

    a. You handle it internally because it has nothing to do with you. Do not take it personally.

    b. Remember, there may come a time when you need a special favor from the leader.

    c. If you feel that you must confront the issue externally, request a one-on-one meeting with the leader or person. Do not make them appear wrong.

    d. Calmly explain how you feel and what you desire. If you still do not get the response you desire, don't take it personally, let it go and move on. Your days of special privileges will come, if you remain positive and motivated.

6. What would you do if the leader of the team were about to make a terrible mistake; moreover, the leader is not interested in hearing your solution?

    a. Put a request for a meeting in writing.

    b. Use this meeting to make your case.

c. If, after the meeting, you still don't feel satisfied that your concerns were taken seriously, write a follow-up memo that reflects what was discussed in the meeting. In some cases, you may want to copy to the superior of the leader, but only if the issue is critical.

d. Continue to support the leader in their final decision.

7. How do you effectively communicate to someone that they are wrong, without making them feel wrong or stupid?

a. First make sure you are correct in your information.

b. Next, whether it is in a meeting or one on one, start with a similar mistake you made in the past, explain the parallel and then offer your proposed answer or solution.

c. If they respond defensively, simply apologize. Tell them your intent was not to offend but to help them by learning from your mistake. It could save you some time and energy. And move on.

8. How do you confront someone who has overstepped your boundary?

a. Calm down, so that you can think clearly before reacting.

b. Do not take it personally, because it will only make you more upset.

c. Be clear that you are going to come out of this situation victoriously.

d. Finally, verbally communicate to the attacker that they have overstepped your boundary and that you would appreciate it if they would stop because it is beginning to annoy you.

9. What should you do when you are not going to meet a deadline for a project?

> ➢ Put it in writing that you are not going to meet your "ABC" deadline on "ABCD" project.
> ➢ Do not forget to put in the memo when you will have the "ABCD" project completed and in their hands.

10. What should you do if someone asks you to do something unethical?

  a. Explain to the person that what they are asking you to do would be unethical and that you do not want a backlash to come back on you.

  b. If the person responds, "Yes, I understand, but I just need you to do it."

  c. Put in a confidential memo/email to the person, "As per your request, I am executing ABCD. If there is anything else I can do, please let me know."

  d. Carbon-copy a superior or human resources and keep a copy safe. You must be able to provide this information immediately; just in case you need verification of the event.

11. What would you do if someone accused you of slander?

  a. Did you give the true facts? If the answer is "yes", then do not feel offended, insecure or doubtful.

  b. Be clear about your motives because it will direct your next move.

  c. Sincerely apologize to your accuser in writing or verbally. Let them know that slander was not your intent. However, these are the facts, as you understand them to be. Please correct me if I am wrong in my information.

12. What should you do when a team member is late giving you documents or information needed to complete your end of the project?

    a. Be certain that you gave them the material they needed in order to complete their end of the project.

    b. Put in a "reminder memo" to the person that they missed ABCD deadline on ABCD project. Tell them you need the information immediately or ask them to provide a date when they will have the information in your hands.

    c. In some cases you may need to copy their superior.

    d. If they disrespect you by not responding, don't disrespect yourself by not sending another "reminder memo" to them and their superior.

13. What should you do when a team member becomes your enemy? How should you protect yourself?

    a. Deal with it internally first. Meditate on how you are going to transform this negative situation into a positive one.

    b. Perception is reality. If you don't like your reality, then change your perception to reflect the reality you desire. Do not speak negatively about the enemy/person.

    c. Perceive them as your teacher and decide to learn how to be a more powerful person/team player. This will empower you to transform your enemies into your allies.

14. How should you deal with a team member who acts superior and treats you as if you are inferior?

    a. Red flag. We teach people how to treat us by how we treat ourselves.

b. People can only disrespect and belittle you if you allow them to. Do not allow them to control how you feel about yourself.

c. Focus your energy on doing something that will help you in reaching your highest potential.

d. When you are in their presence and they are acting out, learn to be emotionless around them. Show them what real power is by not responding to their ignorance. It works every time.

15. What should you do if you fear telling a team member the truth?

a. Decide to tell the truth because if you do not, it will continue to steal your energy.

b. Evaluate what you expect to lose if you tell the truth (Power, Love, Respect, Money). Remember, you have all of those elements within you, so you can never lose them.

c. Write a letter to explain, "I lied and I realize that I have to tell you the truth. And the reason I lied was because I did not want to disappoint you." Or, do not give an excuse. "I apologize for not telling you the truth and hope that you can forgive me."

d. Leave it up to them to "Do the right thing". If they forgive you, great. If they do not forgive you, it is still great because you did your part and that is all you can do.

16. What should you do when someone loses patience with you?

a. Calm down and do not take it personally. Their frustration, usually, has very little to do with you.

b. Be patient with the attacker because you want people to be patient with you.

c. Calmly ask the attacker, "Can we take a break because I can see that you are losing patience with me and I will not work under those conditions."

d. Or let them be impatient, without allowing it to steal your energy or slow you down.

17. How do you get people to do what you desire, without intimidating or manipulating them?

a. First, you must be at the top of your game. People notice and respect people who are powerful, professional and strive for excellence. This is shown by work performance, not by telling people you are powerful.

b. Now, you are ready to present a strong case to team members. They will listen because they are already aware of your quest for excellence.

18. What is the responsibility of the team leader?

a. The team leader is responsible for getting the right people on the bus and the wrong people off the bus.

b. The team leader is responsible for clarifying the goals and objectives of the team and making sure the team says on tract.

c. They also are responsible for inspiring their team members to their highest potential and possibility.

19. What should you do when you have made a mistake with a team member?

a. It is important to acknowledge the mistake to the team member.

b. Next, you should apologize for the error.

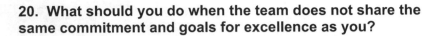
20. What should you do when the team does not share the same commitment and goals for excellence as you?

    a. Ask yourself the question. "Am I truly committed to excellence or am I just looking for an excuse to not perform at my highest level?"

    b. Consciously decide to leave that team and find another team that shares your same commitment and goals for excellence.

    c. Don't wait until your situation becomes unbearable before you decide to leave.

Affirm:

I Am Powerful Enough

To Fulfill My Purpose and Achieve
the Love, Joy, Peace & Great Riches
I Truly Desire and Deserve!

Daily Renewal

BY MARVIN MACK
YOUR PERSONAL & PROFESSIONAL
DEVELOPMENT COACH

THE CENTER FOR MIND & ESTEEM DEVELOPMENT, INC.

13 Daily Renewals to Discover Your Inner Power

Table of Contents

Copyright © by Marvin Mack
The Center For Mind & Esteem Development, Inc.
15 Charles Plaza
Baltimore, MD 21201
Iampowerfulenough.com
410-385-8978

Intention

Who do you desire to be and what do you desire to create with the rest of your life?

Health - Power Conscious Goal #1:

> **I intend to achieve a healthier, stronger mind, body and spirit.**

Relationships - Power Conscious Goal #2:

> **I intend to create successful relationships with all people, both personally and professionally.**

Professional Advancement - Power Conscious Goal #3:

> **I intend to achieve professional advancement.**

Financial Wealth - Power Conscious Goal #4:

> **I intend to achieve financial wealth.**

Authentic Success - Power Conscious Goal #5:

> **I intend to achieve the love, joy, peace and great riches I truly desire and deserve.**

Decide Now

1. I decide now to **look beyond negative appearances** and seek the truth. Mastering this concept will empower me to discover how profoundly powerful I am to transform negative appearances into positive truths.

2. I decide now to **relax and be patient** with myself and people, while at the same time, doing what must be done in order to materialize my deepest goals and desires. Mastering this concept will empower me to re-energize, think more clearly and take the necessary action steps required in order to achieve my daily objectives.

3. I decide now to **listen to my intuition** and follow through on what it tells me to do. This will allow me to tap into a higher level of intelligence in order to materialize my deepest goals and desires.

4. I decide now to **take back the power** that I have given to negative people, situations or circumstances. Mastering this concept will allow me to re-focus my time, energy and thoughts on materializing my highest potential and possibility. I now realize that I have the power enough to fulfill my purpose and create a great life.

5. I decide now to **take risks and never give up** on discovering how profoundly powerful I am to set goals and do what must be done in order to bring those goals into physical manifestation. I am powerful enough. I am Powerful enough to make effective decisions that will support me in materializing my deepest goals and desires.

5 Realizations for Action

Moving from an Understanding to Action

1. **I now realize that I must** Operate At My Highest Potential **on a daily basis in order to grow and develop my mind, body and spirit.**

2. **I realize that I must** Think Powerfully **in order to overcome my life challenges to Succeed.**

3. **I now realize that I must** Believe and have Confidence **in my ability to "do what must be done" in order to successfully complete my daily objectives.**

4. **I now realize that I must** Make Effective Decisions **on a daily basis. This will support the achievement of my deepest goals and desires.**

5. **I now realize that I must** Take Action Now **if my deepest intent is to materialize my personal and professional goals and desires.**

At this level of Power Conscious thinking, ultimately you will be motivated to discover the power within to "Do What Must Be Done" in order to materialize your goals and desires.

5 Power Conscious Attitudes For Success Now
I Can! I Will! It is Done!
I Give Thanks!

1. I can and I will **forgive myself and other people** for any wrongdoings. This will allow me to be open and receptive to Healing and Transforming my life beyond my wildest dreams. I Give Thanks!

2. I can and I will **believe and have confidence in my ability to operate at my highest potential** in order to create love, joy, peace and great riches on this earth. I Give Thanks!

3. I can and I will **react and respond to life powerfully,** regardless of what life puts before me. This will empower me to react and respond to life powerfully in order to create the great life I truly desire and deserve. Not just for myself, but for all the people on this planet. I Give Thanks!

4. I can and I will **stop allowing negative people, situations and circumstances to drain my energy** and take me off focus. I will re-focus that energy on realizing my highest potential to materialize my deepest goals and desires. I Give Thanks!

5. I can and I will **attract into my life positive people, situations and circumstances** that reflect and support my deepest goals and desires. In addition, I can and I will attract the love, joy, peace and great riches I truly desire and deserve. I Give Thanks!

I Surrender To My Higher Power

I Surrender To A Higher Power Within Myself

BE STILL AND KNOW THAT I AM POWERFUL

I am open and receptive to **discovering a higher power** within myself in order to achieve my highest Potential and Possibility.

I **forgive myself and other people** for any wrongdoings; therefore, I am free from guilt, shame and resentment.

I am open and receptive to **learning all that life has to teach** me, so that I am a stronger, more powerful person.

I am open and receptive to using my inner power to **heal and transform** my life to achieve my heart's desires.

I am open and receptive to overcoming my life challenges to **achieve the love, joy, peace and great riches** I truly desire and deserve.

I am open and receptive to overcoming my fears, doubts and insecurities, to **do what must be done** in order to **manifest my desires.**

I am open and receptive to **being a powerful person** to give great service and achieve my personal and professional goals and desires.

I Surrender To A Higher Power Within Myself!
BE STILL AND KNOW THAT I AM POWERFUL
I Give Thanks. I Give Thanks. I Give Thanks.

I Am The Presence and the Power of Love

I Love Myself Unconditionally – My love for myself is not regulated by my successes, failures or who likes me or not. I love myself unconditionally because I am unconditional love. At this level of empowerment, I attract and draw to myself the love, joy, peace and great riches I truly desire and deserve.

I Am Responsible for My Life – I take full responsibility for healing and transforming my life to achieve my personal and professional goals and desires.

I Am Perfect Health – Every bone, muscle, tissue and cell of my body is filled with love and perfection. Therefore, I am eternally youthful, beautiful and in perfect health.

I Am Forgiving – I forgive myself and other people for any wrongdoings; therefore, I am free from guilt, shame and resentment. I have learned the lesson and now I am prepared to go to my next level of love, joy, peace and prosperity.

I Am Standing on Solid Ground – I am powerful enough to stop allowing negative people, situations and circumstances to have power and control over me. Therefore, there is nothing or no one that can stop me from loving, believing and having confidence in myself.

I Only Have Loving Relationships With Everyone (Family, Friends, Enemies, The World) - I love, respect and appreciate myself; therefore, I treat everyone with love and respect. I no longer feel the need to please people or understand why they do what they do. I accept people for who they are because I know who I Am. I give Love. I give Love. I give Love.

I Am Living my Life On Purpose – My main purpose is to discover how profoundly powerful I am to create Love, Joy, Peace and Great Riches in this world.

I Am Free, Free, Free – I am free because I know who I am, and I know that I can do all things with love that supports and strengthens me. Now, I operate at my fullest potential to achieve my personal and professional goals and desires.

In the name of Love, I am Love and I am willing to see and experience Love in this world.

I Am The Greatest

I Feel Great
I Look Great
I Am Great

I Am Powerful – I am spiritually, mentally and physically strong enough to overcome my life challenges to achieve my goals and desires. I am powerful enough to fulfill my purpose and achieve the love, joy, peace and great riches I truly desire and deserve!

I Am Intelligent - I have the brainpower to create, orchestrate and manifest greatness in my life. I learn and master any information or skill because I am a thinker and I use my brain to think. My mind is strong enough to visualize and manifest anything that my heart desires.

I Am Courageous – I fear nothing or no one. I am the presence and the power of love. Love is the most powerful force on earth. Therefore, I am powerful enough to overcome my fears, doubts and insecurities to achieve my heart's desires. I can do all things with love that supports and strengthens me.

I Am Unique – I am a special individual expression of love. Only I can do things the way that I do them. I add something extra special to this world.

I Am Beautiful – I am beautiful because I am the Presence and the Power of Love.

I Am The Greatest

I Feel Great! I Look Great! I Am Great!

I Give Thanks!

4 Powerful Affirmations to Boost Your Energy Level

1. I have an unlimited amount of energy.

When you start to feel overwhelmed by daily tasks, saying this affirmation will relax your mind, freeing you of stress and worry. This relief will allow you to re-focus, regain your power and do what needs to be done in order to move your life forward.

2. I am a powerful force of energy.

When you are faced with negative forces or obstacles coming against you, saying this affirmation will empower your mind to focus on solutions to overcome the challenge. When your mind is empowered, it feels equipped and strong enough to conquer the world to achieve its goals.

3. I can, I will. It is done.

When you start feeling frustrated because you failed or are heading in that direction, saying this affirmation will restore your belief and self-confidence. Affirming and knowing your capability will motivate and give you the energy to push forward until you succeed.

4. I can do anything.

When you start to feel as though you cannot do something, or a project seems overwhelming, saying this affirmation will empower your mind to get the job done. When you think positive thoughts and have a good attitude, you are tapping into a powerful source of energy that will help you to achieve your goals.

I Am Empowered

a. I plan, manage and organize myself to focus, execute, meet deadlines and achieve my daily goals and objectives.

b. I present and communicate myself confidently and effectively to get what I need from people.

c. I am mentally, emotionally and physically strong enough to overcome my life challenges, such as: multiple projects, energy crises and negative people.

d. I react and respond to all conflicts in a powerful manner.

e. I give quality service in a professional manner to be successful now.

f. I enjoy harmonious relationships with everyone: family, friends, enemies, and the world.

g. I love, respect and appreciate myself. I believe in myself. I believe that I will materialize my goals and desires.

h. I am open and receptive to discovering my highest potential to achieve the love, joy, peace and great riches I truly desire and deserve.

i. I am Energy. I am Passion. I am Free. I Am Empowered

j. I give thanks. I give thanks. I give thanks.

Affirm 5 Leadership Principles for The Successful Leader

1. **LEAD - I am responsible for providing great service and achieving the goals and objectives of my company.**

2. **LEAD - I present and communicate myself powerfully with integrity.**

3. **LEAD – My top priority is to empower team members to operate at their fullest potential.**

4. **LEAD - I Have the Emotional Fortitude – to be "listenable" and to effectively confront negative people and situations directly, and accept full responsibility for the outcome.**

5. **LEAD - In the face of challenges, I retain faith that my team and I will prevail in the end, not weakened but stronger.**

Know Yourself
A Tip for Developing Good Presentation & Communication Skills

"Know The Answers To the Following Questions Before Any
Interview or Presentation"

To Present Powerfully Is A Self-Discover Process

1. Who are you?
I am powerful, intelligent, courageous, unique and beautiful. (How does this get played out in your daily life?)

2. What is your purpose in this world?
My purpose is to be a great person and to share that greatness with this world. (How do you go about sharing your greatness with this world?)

3. What are you personal and professional goals and desires?
I desire to:
    a. Develop a stronger Mind, Body and Spirit
    b. Develop Loving Relationships with all people
    c. Advance Professionally and
    d. Increase my financial net worth

4. How do you overcome your life challenges?
I effectively overcome my life challenges in a powerful manner. (Give an example.)

5. How should you present and communicate yourself in the world? I Present and Communicate myself to the world in a Loving and Powerful manner.

I Am Powerful Enough

Self-Management Affirmations

1. I Know My 4 Top Priorities

2. I Forgive, let it go, and move on

3. I Stand In the Consciousness Level Of Success

4. I Just Do It "Now"

5. I Don't Take "Negative Attacks" Personally and I Don't Get Emotional about them

6. I Observe The Signs, Listen to My Intuition & Plan Accordingly

7. I am not into Self-Promotion; I Let My Work Speak For Itself

8. I Clarify, Confirm & Always Follow-Up and Follow-Through

9. I Set The Example Of Success, Regardless of my position in life

10. I Let People Know Where I Stand by Affirming My Rules of Engagement

11. I Speak to People Directly and Let It Go

12. I Know When to Stand-Down and I Know When to Stand Up For Myself

13. I Have Stopped being a "People Pleaser"

14. I Believe people when they show me who they are

10 Powerful Affirmations for Professional Advancement

1. I Treat All People with Love and Respect

2. I take personal responsibility for my success and failures!

3. I handle all challenges in a powerful manner!

4. I only participate in conversations that are empowering.

5. I treat all people fairly and equally.

6. I accept constructive criticism and strive to be better and better!

7. I am a "take charge" person and take responsibility for completing my workload!

8. I am genuinely happy when other people are promoted or succeed – even when I am not.

9. I always give more than expected.

10. I only speak the highest truth that I know.

Dear Friend,

Thank You.

As we affirm and internalize these simple but powerful words and concepts, ultimately we will discover the power within to heal and transform our lives to fulfill our purpose and achieve the love, joy, peace and great riches you truly desire and deserve.

Please always remember, we are the presences and the power of Love and love is the most powerful force on earth. Therefore, we can do all things with love that supports and strengthens us.

Now empower yourself to create the great life you have the potential live.

Enjoy.

Marvin Mack, Founder and Director of
The Center For Mind & Esteem Development, Inc.
Your Personal & Professional Development Coach